Madison Cooper

MADISON COOPER

by

MARION TRAVIS

WORD BOOKS, Publisher

Waco, Texas

Contents

Preface

LIKE ALL GOOD novelists, Madison Cooper was many men in one, yet in my early research I did not meet a contemporary of the man who warmly volunteered that he liked the sometimes controversial writer-philanthropist. Therefore, I concluded, once my research began in 1964, that he deliberately kept all people at arm's length, if not estranged. Then as more time passed, I realized that he had many admirers, but they were hardy souls whose admiration asked little in return.

I do not think I could have loved Madison Cooper, because the lovable in him was far beneath the surface. However, I admire his grit. He was a fighter. His battles had nothing to do with fists or guns; they called for mental and moral derring-do, and this he had in great quantities. He was somebody special in a time (chaotic twentieth century), place (economically depressed, often timid Central Texas), and circumstance (born rich) that could have pummeled him into a paper-thin nobody.

Instead he pointed the way to human understanding and to a better future for his fellow citizens in Waco with an effectiveness that thrums through time. The lesson is there for all to learn.

This is meant to be a fair and honest story, and I hope the reader will use information in these pages to weave a Madison Cooper of his own.

Primary source material from the Cooper Foundation collection provided me with most information in these pages. The collection consists of the permanent files accumulated by Madison Cooper. Interestingly, Cooper early formed the habit of keeping carbon copies of all his business and personal correspondence; thus the collection includes letter sequences that convey important episodes in his life.

To Madison Cooper, any lie, however trifling, was immoral; and being independent both by nature and circumstance, he indulged himself in a lifetime of morality as he saw it. This sharp line between the real and imagined is significant in a complete picture of the man, and an invaluable aid to the biographer.

7

Foremost among generous people who helped me in this work was the late Robert Bradley Hoover, my good friend, who for three and one-half years helped sustain the faith I needed in myself to do a difficult job. He joined me in the resolve that the typescript would truly portray Madison Cooper, within the restrictions of evolving a man from words spoken, and on paper, to more words on paper. Brad Hoover died January 7, 1968, and the absence of his counsel is a great loss to all of his friends.

The late Hilton E. Howell, attorney and civic-education leader, and other trustees of the Cooper Foundation filled an important role by granting me exclusive access to the Cooper Foundation collection and other materials until my work was complete. The foundation placed no restrictions on conclusions I drew about Madison Cooper.

I am glad to note the role of the *Waco Tribune-Herald* which allowed me leaves of absence from my duties there. Especially am I grateful to the editor-in-chief of Newspapers, Inc., Harry M. Provence, himself a fine writer, who labored as my editor in the final stages to help me bring the story out of the rhetorical woods and maze of material.

Madison Cooper's sister, Mrs. Walter G. Lacy, provided me with valuable insights into her brother's childhood; and one of her sons, Lawrence C. Lacy, was most helpful when he joined his mother in providing me with information unavailable except from members of Madison Cooper's family.

I recall with pleasure interviews with many of Madison Cooper's Waco friends, professional advisers, and employees. Their recollections and interpretations helped me get perspective on my subject. For such help I am indebted to Dr. Boyd Alexander, the late E. Y. Boynton, Mrs. C. J. Cartwright, Roger N. Conger, Walter B. Dossett, Miss Mary Farrell, Mrs. H. G. Fulbright, Raymond Goddard, Mrs. Manton Hannah and the late Mr. Hannah, the late Hilton E. Howell, Hollis King, Miss Lalla Fae Lacy, Leland G. McCullough, W. W. Naman, Mrs. Herman Olenbush and the late Mr. Olenbush,

Miss Mildred Rast, Robert Radle, the late Mrs. William Sloane, and Mrs. Bertha Lee Walton. Useful material from Dr. K. P. Wittstruck, Capt. Tom Bennett, Albert Fortune, and J. L. Mayfield helped me provide the full account of Madison Cooper's death.

With appreciation I acknowledge the kind permission of these teachers and other associates of Madison Cooper who approved publication of their personal or business correspondence in this volume: Austin Olney, Paul Brooks, and Lovell Thompson, all of Houghton Mifflin Co. in Boston, Mass.; Mack Gorham of New York City; Edward Hodnett of Midland, Mich.; and the family of the late Rev. C. T. Caldwell.

MARION TRAVIS

Waco, Texas, 1971

I Introduction

SUDDEN PASSING IS . . . in every way the best sort of leave-taking." These were Madison Alexander Cooper, Jr.'s own words in a condolence note he sent to Mrs. Frederick Lewis Allen when her husband, the editor and historian, died.[1]

Two years later the same words could have been applied to Cooper if any truly bereft person had been left behind to write them. But there was no one to grieve profoundly Madison Cooper's quick death. As always, he was alone.

Conspicuously, privately, in truth, and in legend, he was his own man all his life. That is the way he wanted it. He never let anyone beyond his parents get close to him. He was alone September 28, 1956, at Waco Municipal Stadium where he jogged around the red cinder track the last time. He walked to his old Packard automobile, his heart failed, and he died.

It was typical that Madison Cooper *ran* his last mile. Most people remember him as always in a hurry, as a boy and as a man.

Striking testimony to this man's impact on his community appeared the following morning. The *Waco News-Tribune* with a five-column, two-line headline in bold type shouted from the top of page one. Madison Cooper had been found dead at Municipal Stadium. Illustrating the long obituary was a Bob Ponder photograph that Cooper himself had once satirically dubbed "The Thinker." It had been widely distributed by Houghton Mifflin Company of Boston and published across the land in 1952 when businessman Cooper became a best-selling author. Cooper tagged the picture to keep it separate from another by Ponder, an equally well-known pose Cooper privately called "The Streetwalker's Hamlet."

Newspapers and other periodicals all over the nation and in Europe published the Cooper obituary. Among them were *Time,* the *New York Times,* and *Publishers' Weekly.*

Morning newspaper readers in Waco learned that the funeral would consist of a brief graveside service at twelve noon, September 29—less than twenty hours after his heart stopped beating. Through the grapevine they heard that every detail of the funeral was planned

and written out for the undertaker by Cooper himself nine years
earlier, in 1947. In similar fashion his mother had planned her own
funeral, but instead of typing her special plans she passed them on
to her daughter and son. They had carried them out in 1939.

Like his mother, Madison Cooper did not want to be embalmed.
And he wrote, "After preparation for burial, my body is to be
viewed by no one except as may be necessary for legal proof of
death. I do not approve of the exhibition of the remains of anyone."
The original copy of the funeral instructions was put in the care of
Bertha Lee Walton, his cook and housekeeper. Robert Bradley
Hoover, manager of Cooper's properties, made things happen as
Cooper directed from the typed memorandum composed during his
lifetime.

"Mr. Madison always wanted to be buried like a soldier. He told
me this," Bertha later recalled. The funeral instructions verify her
memory:

> 3. Since I want my body to become part of the earth as quickly as
> possible, my wishes are: . . . That my body be dressed in my own
> clothing (dark suit and tie, white shirt); wrapped in blankets, preferably
> Army OD, and interred without coffin or vault of any kind. If a coffin
> is legally required, use an unpainted wooden box of the least ex-
> pensive material and construction.

So read part of one item on a twelve-item memorandum.

No procession, no chairs, no tent, no flowers, only simplicity and
brevity. Just to hold the funeral cost low? Perhaps—in part. It is no
secret that he could find ways to cut costs that made skinning a flint
look like squeezing grapes. But to say that Madison Cooper was
avaricious, or mean, was never true. A better reason than niggardli-
ness for the simplicity of his funeral was his profound distaste for
ordinary pretense. He scorned show of sentimentality.

This is not to say Madison Cooper, Jr., did not bloom socially
with the best of them. As a young man he loved parties and dances.
Always he knew how to be charming. His company manners were
his private code. When on his best behavior, his voice carried patrician
Southern accents untouched by the drawling slur of small-town
Texans. One knows this sound if he has heard an Anglican bishop
from Atlanta, or a Richmond industrialist, or a Winston-Salem banker.
Cooper lost this speech in anger. At such times his pitch rose, the
usual crisp speed doubled, and he even stuttered in annoyance.

When he was young, he wore modish, expensive men's fashions on social occasions. When he was older, he turned to old clothes for his working attire and he was called eccentric. Yet on evenings out he always conformed to the style of the day—with suits from the rack. The adult Madison Cooper never dressed to suggest his net worth.

His balanced, well-proportioned features made him handsome all his life. Brown hair with red highlights eventually gave way to some greying, which he covered with dye. He was tall, slender, well formed, and manly.

The adult Cooper made his daily rounds to the bank, his downtown buildings, and other locations carrying a brown leather brief case. He always had many irons in the fire. Inside the brief case he carried memoranda and pertinent data on rents to be collected (he owned through purchase and inheritance many downtown business properties and Central Texas farms), books to be rented (his eyes consumed them by the shelfful all his life), bills to be paid, debts to collect, or the thousand and one other details of managing his multifarious business, investment, and writing affairs. When the brief case aged and frayed, he continued to get service from it. This was part of his method for handling complex affairs without a secretary or a staff of assistants. Fortunately, Brad Hoover and *Sironia, Texas* came along at about the same time. The former handled the property and business details as the latter expanded Cooper's career in new directions.

Cooper had a special envelope near Miss Mildred Rast's desk in the Citizens National Bank where she put any mail or messages for him. Pud Rast was secretary to Walter G. Lacy, Jr., bank president and Cooper's nephew. About once yearly the envelope showed wear from its service, and if Miss Rast didn't change it when he wasn't around, he would advise her to patch it up and make do. He was one of the bank's largest stockholders.

He came into the bank one day dressed in the old clothes he liked to wear when working or walking in downtown Waco. Miss Rast glanced at, then looked away from, the big hole torn in the back of Cooper's trousers. Describing it later, she gestured at her upper right thigh.

"I wrote him a little note, thinking it would embarrass him if I told him out loud."

"Your skin is exposed."

Cooper took the note and headed toward the bank lobby, then stopped. Peeling off his favorite sweater with the leather patch elbows, he put it around his waist and tied the arms together in front—as a backwards apron. This arrangement hid the hole.

Cooper returned to the bank president's secretary's desk. He looked serious and she was a little startled. Leaning over, he stage-whispered into her ear:

"I'm going to do something nice for you. When you get a hole in your britches, I'm going to lend you my sweater."

Miss Rast is one of the few people to guess accurately that, as a mature man, Cooper led two lives. One was the paradoxically pinch-penny philanthropist in Waco. This Madison Cooper deliberately fed the seething local legends of his parsimony, while demanding complete anonymity for his ever broadening beneficence to the city and "deserving" individuals.

The other was a fun-loving young charmer—a side of his personality which stayed with him to the end. When it emerged in letters or conversations during his latter years, it seemed startling and unreal to old friends who had weakened under the strains of their lives. This Madison Cooper went to a spa in Battle Creek, Michigan, in 1925 when he was thirty-one years old:

I dashed around with beauties varying from thirty-five to thirteen . . . I put on balloon pants and left off garters with the best of 'em. There was no one around to check on me, and I always argue that a vacation is a vacation . . . Drove from Battle Creek to New York City. Saw lots of shows.

Later in New York he made friends with literary and theatrical people. Throughout the last twenty-five years of his life he sometimes spent as much as a month each year taking in Broadway, the clubs, and visiting briefly with people in New York and other East Coast locations. He vastly admired people of talented accomplishment, wished to be recognized as one himself, and frequently opened opportunities for other Texans to develop their talents. At the age of fifty-seven he was able to show them the way by his own example. At last the "other side" of Madison Cooper, humanist and writer, was revealed although misunderstood. He blossomed as the author of a national best seller, a spectacular novel—*Sironia, Texas*. It had been written at home secretly over a period of eleven years.

With people he liked, Madison Cooper, Jr., was scrupulously

patient, understanding. He tried to curb the caustic retort. He left the cold shoulder and eccentricity at home. But he didn't leave behind his respect for the well-spent dollar.

Yet when the end of his life approached, it was not the good times on the East Coast or the Texas literary scene that pulled at his affections. It was Waco. Wanting to draw more benefits of civilization to his Texas hometown, he established the Cooper Foundation "to make Waco, Texas, a better or more desirable city in which to live." Waco was the sole beneficiary of his three million dollar estate. It was a grand gesture from a man who frankly never established an easy, friendly rapport with his hometown. And as much money as he gave away personally, he rarely gave it with Santa Claus beneficence. He had a way of wanting to know if it were well spent.

Cooper's compulsion to give was only slightly stronger than his drive to get. If the last hadn't been a commanding impulse, the first could have amounted to little. He spread himself thin over a fantastic variety of interests.

II Growing Up

LONG AGO I accepted the idea that everybody is largely the result of all that's gone before, even before he was born. Something like the ingredients of my turtle broth!" Cooper had his Miss Milly Thaxton say in *Sironia, Texas.* ". . . I still believe 'folks' as you say determine how high-minded and capable one can be, but how near he gets to what he *can* be depends on two other things, his surroundings and himself."

Soon after these words appeared in print, the author, who believed them true, wrote to an Arkansawyer, "I am proud indeed, of the Roane blood [his mother's side of the house]. My paternal grandparents were from North Carolina and (disregarding such trivia as mathematics) I like to feel that I am 50% Arkansan, 50% North Carolinian, and 100% Texan."

John Selden Roane was Madison's maternal grandfather, and the fourth man elected governor of Arkansas. Earlier, he read law in Arkansas, led a regiment in the Mexican War, and fought a bloodless duel with Albert Pike, according to Harnett Kane in *Gentlemen, Swords, and Pistols.* Kane's account says the dueling scene was on a sand bar on the Arkansas River in Indian Territory opposite Fort Smith. The issue was Pike's claim that Roane mishandled Arkansas troops in the Mexican War.

To show his disdain for Roane, Pike calmly puffed a fresh cigar. With seconds and physicians, both men fired and missed. Pike lit a second cigar; the seconds conferred; Roane called for another shot; they missed again. This exhausted the patience of the seconds and the doctors who stopped the proceedings by threatening to leave. Then if either man were wounded, he would have to bleed to death.

Roane's second authorized one doctor to say, "Our principal has declared himself as having received entire satisfaction." There was more maneuvering to save face and the incident closed in Fort Smith where all exchanged toasts. Roane was elected governor soon afterwards.

The governor married Mary Kimbrough Smith, a beautiful brunette from North Carolina. Among their four children was Martha Dillon Roane, born in 1861, the same year her father went off to war as a Confederate officer. He came home a brigadier general, but lived only two years afterward. His widow took her children back to Tulip, Arkansas, to live with her parents. There she reared her family to believe that the purpose of life was to attain the puritanical state of grace, a code of stiff morals considered pleasing to God. In a few years she had to call on all the strength of her religious convictions, for her parents died leaving her alone with the children. The widow Roane, a Baptist turned Presbyterian, wore mourning clothing the rest of her long life. Her only jewelry was a shiny gold breastpin containing a photograph of the governor.

Martha Dillon Roane, called Mattie and Matt, upheld family pride as did her mother; furthermore, she believed and practiced the stern requirements of her mother's Presbyterian religion.

On his father's side, Madison was descended from Joseph Smith, an Englishman from Bristol who came to the American colonies in 1632 to settle in Kings and Queens County, Virginia. Samuel Smith II, a grandson, served under General Wolfe during the French and Indian War, which precipitated a significant development in family history: he received about three thousand acres of land, through Lord Granville, in Granville County, North Carolina.

Among many Smith descendants reared on the ancestral acres (some went to Arkansas) was Anne Smith Downey who married an Englishman, James Crawford Cooper. To them was born a boy, Alexander, whose five children would include Madison Alexander Cooper born near Oxford in Granville County, North Carolina, in 1856. Known all his life as Matt, this Cooper by the age of nineteen was ready to assert his independence of father and stepmother, and he did so by heading for Texas. His mother, Harriett Young Cooper, died when he was fourteen.

Waco, with the only bridge at the time on the Brazos River, which cuts the eastern third of Texas off from the rest, was a gateway to the frontier. It was also a new railroad center in 1874. Here young Matt Cooper found a job as night clerk at the Pacific Hotel. In that role he scanned the raw town for opportunity. The work he settled on, peddling apples and potatoes in a wagon pulled by a mule, may appear puny and commonplace to the twentieth-century mind, but it was a sound move in the 1870s in Waco with its mud streets and jerry-built stores around the square. Many of them were

brick, but the architecture and construction approached amateurishness. The triumph of the time was to get a building up that would
admit people and keep out cold and rain.

Waco had got off to a poor start in 1849 with a weak government
that lost its corporation soon afterwards. For about ten years before
Matt Cooper came to town there existed no city government at all.
In its place was a motley and growing accumulation of people representing every human type and cherishing every popular principle
advanced in Western civilization for a hundred years. It was to this
chaotic mass of Americans and foreigners that Matt Cooper was
attracted. He saw a city in the making, and he rightly determined
that food would furnish him with a fortune.

In 1880 he advanced to his own hole-in-the-wall wholesale produce business on the north side of the square. He lived in the same
quarters and boarded at the nearby Taylor House. Concurrently,
Waco began behaving like a city. First ranching, then Brazos Valley
and blacklands cotton farming pumped commercial strength into
the town which, even so, remained on the economic frontier of the
state for many years. Indian depredations were still a problem in
Texas when Matt Cooper came to Waco.

Following a visit to North Carolina, and through relatives in
Arkansas, Matt Cooper met and loved Martha Dillon Roane. She
came from his kind of people—similar geographical background,
mutual relatives. He convinced her that she belonged in Waco, and
she believed in him so warmly that she ran away from her family
in Tulip to marry him in a home ceremony in Holden, Missouri.
Martha was twenty-six years old; Matt was thirty-three. It may be
said that at the age of twenty-six Miss Mattie should not have to
run away from home to marry, but that is the way it was, because
she had long been the strong, good-humored, and independent member of her family and her closest kin needed her at home. The
wedding took place in the home of their mutual relatives, the Duvals.

This was in 1888 and Matt A. Cooper's name appeared in the
Waco City Directory the following year in capital letters. Such a
designation attested to his stature in the business community, for
by this time his wholesale produce house had expanded to a double-
front on North Fourth Street. He offered his retailers a variety of
fruit and other produce: apples, onions, potatoes, cabbage, sour (*sic*)
kraut, butter, cheese, pickles, pigs' feet, vinegar, apple cider, dried
apples, lemons, oranges, beans, and peanuts. Add some of these foods

to frontier bread, beef, and gravy and out comes an uptown full meal.

A man of local importance, M. A. Cooper, as he was now called, became a director of the Waco National Bank. He worked from daylight until past dark six days a week at his wholesale business. Breakfast and lunch he had at home, but at night he munched at his desk the sandwiches made by his thrifty wife.

The newlyweds lived at a first class boarding house on North Fifth Street across from St. Paul's Episcopal Church. They lived there when their first child was born in 1889. Mrs. Cooper named the baby girl for Owen Meredith's Lucile, heroine of a highly popular narrative poem by the same name. Their second child, Christine, was born in 1891.

In 1892 M. A. Cooper bought out the wholesale grocery business of the five Moore brothers and painted on the front of the building at the corner of South Fourth and Mary: M. A. Cooper and Co.

The Cooper family's first house was a green frame cottage of seven rooms at 915 Washington Street. It was among the earliest Waco residences to have a telephone. Even more a source of pride at this house was its indoor bathroom off the side porch, another rarity in a town where most houses had outhouses.

Their third and last child, Madison Alexander Cooper, Jr., was born prematurely June 3, 1894, Jefferson Davis's birthday, at the cottage on Washington Street. The baby cried so hard he turned blue. This was the beginning of a troublesome period of undefined ill health that plagued the boy for several years.

The winds of unkind portion blew strong in the life of Martha Roane Cooper in baby Madison's birth year, 1894, a fact which helps account for her special, lifelong affection for her son. That was the year that her only brother was run over by a train in Arkansas and died slowly. Hugh Roane's death hurt his, and Mattie's, mother so much that for a while the family thought she would lose her sanity. Mattie, with three young children, was called on to supply the will to overcome family grief.

Added to this heartbreak was the death of Mattie's second child. Three-year-old Christine died in 1894 when Madison was six months old. The baby boy, born strong of will and demanding, got his way with his overburdened mother who rationalized her indulgence that the heir apparent of his father's growing position in the business community must be nurtured with care, because he

would be needed to uphold her family's renewed place on the upper
level of society. The years in Tulip had been lean and lonely.

Waco in Madison's birth year was becoming citified in ambition
if not in reality for the first time. It now had a number of good
homes and buildings plus an atmosphere of growth, but its government was still weak, all its streets unpaved, and its economy tied
to the cotton market which habitually careened overnight from
big profits to big panics. Thus, change created a wide open atmosphere which in 1894 attracted a vitriolic classicist, William
Cowper Brann, to Waco where he published a successful monthly
news comment pamphlet, the *Iconoclast*.

Brann, a handsome man and articulate writer, was a master of invective who roasted his mountebanks, chosen from the social and
political elite of the world. Also among his many victims were members of the Baptist church and its chief institution of higher learning,
Baylor University in Waco. Brann's objections to Baptist pride were
centered on the school's president, Rufus C. Burleson. Repeatedly and
excessively Brann skewered the school, its students, and its president
in the *Iconoclast,* and he made enemies. Possibly as a result, Brann
was shot in the back in 1898 on a downtown Waco street. Most
people believed for decades that his murder was attributable to his
attacks on Baylor—but this has never been shown conclusively.
Brann killed his assassin, a Waco citizen not directly connected with
Baylor, after receiving his own mortal wounds.

Thus Brann and his sensational end founded a memory of a
hellbent stand for the truth. Additionally, this brilliant writer and
speaker founded a literary tradition in Waco which had flickered inter-
mittently during the still young city's growth. H. L. Mencken of
Baltimore was destined to assume Brann's title, "Master of Invective,"
but few would be more affected by his memory and tradition than
the child born in Waco the year Brann came to town—Madison A.
Cooper, Jr. How he would carry out his role could not be known,
perhaps even to himself, for many years, but it was inevitable that
young Madison would hear all the stories about Brann the Iconoclast, and he appropriated the courage of Brann unto himself.

But this would be in the future; meanwhile, Waco's role as a
wholesaling center for a farming population that far outnumbered
town dwellers burgeoned from 1890. Matt Cooper, the father, had
perceived early the profits coming from wholesaling and within only
five years after his 1892 purchase of Moore Brothers' wholesale

grocery house, he persuaded his friend Ed C. Barrett, also from North Carolina, to join him and H. K. Brewer in founding the Cooper Grocery Company, a corporation chartered for fifty years. So by the time the century turned, Cooper, toughened by the long haul uphill, was a dominant figure in the food business in a proliferating Central Texas population. Waco soon became one of the largest inland cotton markets in the world, and the white staple put money in many pockets. Young Madison at the same time was growing up as a rich brat.

Throughout grade school years Madis (his childhood name) made good marks. He was a quick learner. While fourteen-year-old Lucile was in Milford at a church school, Madis attended Columbus Street Ward School, and the family home was at 1003 Washington. Some of the boys are reported to have called him Little Miss Cooper. The older boys at school also taunted him about his mother washing behind his ears every morning.

Hospital visits for young Madison diminished as he neared the end of his grade school years. His father received this letter postmarked in Chicago.

My dear Papa

Mama and I came up from the hospital this afternoon.
I certainly was glad to get away from there alive.
I am feeling fine have just had a good supper here at the Stratford.
Papa I want to thank you for all you've done for me.
I hope when I am a little older I will be able to help you in lots of ways.

Your affectionate boy,
Madison

Like most of the well-to-do families in Waco before the days of refrigeration and air conditioning, the Cooper menage moved "up north" to summer resorts to escape the Central Texas heat. Each year Mrs. Cooper took Lucile and Madison to spend July and August in the cooling breezes of Michigan (Charlevoix, Petrosky, Ludington) and Wisconsin (Waupaca). These vacations far from Waco further isolated Madison from intimate contact with the other boys of his hometown.

Mr. and Mrs. Cooper decided in 1905 they should build a new

home suitable for the family of a Waco-style big businessman and commissioned architect Glenn Allen to design it. The three-story brick mansion required two years to complete. It reared its towered front at 1801 Austin Avenue, Waco's new silk-stocking street, then suburban territory. One of the Sunday afternoon diversions for Wacoans was to ride the streetcar out to Eighteenth and Austin to see the mansions. On the Cooper corner they would view terra-cotta decorations, in what was called Italian baroque motif, bedizening the tan brick exterior. Concrete garlands, over fifty columns inside and outside (some decorative, some useful), balconies and stained-glass windows competed for the passer-by's interest. Pointing high at the southeast corner and lording it over a red tile roof rose an octagonal cupola with open sides. It was called a tower and one day would be a hideaway for Madison.

Inside the big house were two stairways, two main. entrances, big halls, and eighteen rooms. With its decorative fleurs-de-lis and hand-painted cupids in the parlor, its paneled effects in the reception hall, the structure proclaimed "Merchant Prince." A tricky annunciator system provided communication from the family quarters to the kitchen and carriage house. And a big boiler in the basement provided steam heat through the artfully molded radiators, although every room on two floors had a fireplace. The first step under the porte-cochere was high to provide the ladies an easy step to the porch from horse-drawn carriages.

Matt Cooper at the age of fifty-three in 1907 now had the symbols of success—he was a corporation president, financier, and railroad director; he lived in style; he had a handsome wife (still a lovely brunette at forty-seven, her hair did not grey until past fifty), and attractive children.

When his son Madison was old enough to learn, Matt Cooper taught him everything about business and finance the boy could understand. And again Madison would be different from the others. He was a rich boy, learning to think of money as a means of authority.

Madison's four high-school years started in late 1907. The boys entered the school building by one door, the girls by another. Segregation of the sexes, however, was not practiced in the classroom where forty-minute sessions began at nine in the morning and ended at three in the afternoon. Everyone brought lunch to school and everyone had to take Latin. In Madison's Latin classes, his hand was usually up first to answer questions or recite.

The University of Texas, though only twenty-seven years old when young Madison Cooper rode the Katy one hundred miles to enter, had a rising prestige and a much gayer social reputation than older, church-related schools of the same era in Texas. The Forty Acres, as the university was called, held nearly two thousand students that year. Its few brick buildings sat among a clutter of frame structures needed to house the classes for which the state legislature had not yet provided construction money.

Madison enrolled in September, 1911, and pledged Sigma Alpha Epsilon (Texas Rho), ready to experiment with the man-about-town role. High collar and porkpie hat typified the well-dressed young man's sartorial tastes.

Long afterwards Cooper characterized his college days as "my party-crazy days." He was pleased to report that "outside of my courses, my activity was principally and preoccupiedly SOCIAL. I went to so many parties when I was younger that I find it relatively easy to pass them up now for work."

At this time he wanted to relate to people. He succeeded in the *externals* of society, but he never achieved the first aim. He was a director of the Saturday night Germans (dance parties) and a guest at innumerable fraternity and sorority parties. At Waco during the 1911 Christmas holiday he rose to new heights as a lavish host. The Waco society editor called his Christmas dance at the Cooper home the most elaborate affair of the local season. Tissue paper roses and jonquils entwined in smilax draped the stair banister. Alessandro's orchestra, screened by palmetto palms, played from the wide stair-landing. Heavy white fabric, called "stretcher," covered the floor and the colorful Oriental rugs were rolled up. Two hundred guests came to the ball, including Sigma Alpha Epsilon friends and University of Texas alumni. They danced the waltz and two-step throughout the big reception hall, the pretty parlor, and the bay-windowed dining room. Upstairs in the hall were chairs in tête-à-tête groups.

During Madison's freshman year at the university, Dr. Everett M. Clark of the English department commended the Waco student on his writing, and on the strength of this encouragement Cooper signed up for English II. He later stated plainly that at no time as a college student did he consider writing professionally. He selected English as his major almost as a last resort. Only the colleges of arts, law, medicine, and engineering offered academic majors. He added a minor in business administration in his final years.

Madison found self-expression in such spare time work as fraternity editor, writing chapter reports for the national Sigma Alpha Epsilon magazine, and he briefly joined the staff of the *Coyote,* a campus humor magazine with a breezy, naive style. Characteristics of Cooper's *Coyote* contributions are evident in this quotation:

> On Thursday, the Tummi Acha Sorority held a so-called reception in its almost-house to honor their inevitable grand officers. Everyone was bored beautifully, the purpose of the evening being fully accomplished.

Through college his grades hovered in the upper 5 percent of his class; the only serious deficiency appeared in physical training. He had a muscular coordination problem that prevented his starting or stopping instantly on signal.

As a university senior he was decorations chairman of the all-school Thanksgiving reception.

"Anacrean has a beautiful lilt," a *Cactus* editor published under Cooper's graduation photograph, referring to his reputation for quick repartee and ribaldry. A subcaption, "That's some more of your business," was provided on request by one of his Sigma Alpha Epsilon brothers and roommate, Leland McCullough, who considered Madison a bit nosy.

What the *Cactus* didn't say was that Madison Cooper, Jr., had begun a lifelong love affair with the University of Texas.

He was graduated with a Bachelor of Arts degree in 1915 and headed for Waco and the wholesale grocery career awaiting him. His primary competence: how to have a good time. His primary aim: to be busy and feel important. His assignment: Cooper Grocery Company produce and candy buyer.

III World War One

MATT COOPER, SR., continued as president and general manager of the Cooper Grocery Company, wholesaling its own brand of coffee and spices, and in 1917 became a director of the Citizens National Bank. He was known as an early supporter of the bold, but doomed, plan to navigate the Brazos and was among the first backers of the interurban line connecting Waco and Dallas. He was an investor in Waco and Wall Street stocks and on the board of directors of another railroad, the Cotton Belt.

Madison was being absorbed into the mode of life in Waco when a war in Europe took him away. With millions of other Americans, he warmed to the words of President Woodrow Wilson's famous war message to Congress, April 2, 1917:

> It is a fearful thing to lead this great peaceful country into war, into the most terrible and disastrous of all wars, . . . But the right is more precious than peace, and we shall fight for all the things which we have always carried nearest our hearts— . . . To such a task we can dedicate our lives and our fortunes, everything we are and everything that we have.

This was Madison Cooper, Jr.'s kind of language. He could get into the fight with dignity. He immediately joined a small group of would-be soldiers who drilled on their own at the Waco City Hall. They couldn't wait for the training camps to open. He persuaded Leland McCullough to join him in the soldiering. While this was going on, Congress passed the army draft bill for conscription of ten million men between ages of twenty-one and thirty-one. Registration was to begin July 5, 1917. But before these untrained civilians could become soldiers, officers to lead and train them must themselves be trained. Result: the Ninety-Day Wonder.

Officer training camps sprang up over the whole country. All followed the plan of volunteer instruction camps at Plattsburg, New York, inaugurated in 1914 by Maj. Gen. Leonard Wood. Thousands of American young men applied for officer training, including Cooper and his friend McCullough.

25

They arrived as cadets on May 8, 1917, at Leon Springs, Texas, near San Antonio, to enter First Officers' Training Camp. Training was ninety days of merciless military hazing to toughen the officer material. The rigid, rushed schedule from 6:15 in the morning until 9:15 at night appealed to Cooper. He not only endured the discipline, he thrived on it. Many of the young men could not take the schedule. They put their trunk lockers up for sale, standard acknowledgement of failure. As the glamour of the Air Service beckoned McCullough, Cooper showed the persistence that ran in his family. It was hell, he admitted to his mother as training ended:

Dear Mama,

I am still so tired that I can't write connectedly, so shall say only a little. I am to get my commission all right on August 15. I don't know where I shall be sent yet. . . . The maneuvers were pretty bad, so hot and tiresome, but they are over now. Think I can arrive in Waco the morning of Aug. 16th, but will wire you later,

Aff
Madis

United States Army strength now depended on the National Guard, Regular Army, and National Army. Latter units included the 360th Infantry Regiment at Camp Travis near San Antonio where the new officer from Waco was sent.

Second Lieutenant Madison A. Cooper, Jr., Infantry Officer Reserve Corps, stood six feet, one-half inch tall. His age: twenty-three years. Remarkable good looks, smooth and tanned complexion, erect and slender body—all this made it easy for women to describe him as dashing in uniform. Yet his attitude belied the description. Then as always he was flattered by the attention of women, but they rarely measured up to his standards. For many decades he used a page from *The Phoenix,* literary magazine of the era, as a bookmark in an encyclopedia of business law. The page bore a "Saying of Shadrach the Wise," typifying at once the vein of humor Cooper liked as well as an inbred distrust of the intentions of women: "Forget not, my son, that a Pair of Soulful Eyes, a soft and clinging Palm, and a mouth like Cupid's bow, are often the lure of a Cold proposition." Now he was often caustic and critical. A natural reserve, and the self-assurance of a superior mind, caused him to be labeled conceited.

When division headquarters called for intelligence officer trainees, the regimental colonel noted Lt. Cooper was qualified. This is how he came to travel by train to Riverbank Laboratories near Aurora, Illinois. The intelligence school was at George Fabyan's Riverbank villa and estate on the Fox River. With other officers, Cooper lived at Hotel Aurora with tight secrecy in force. No one communicated outside the group. They learned to decode messages without a cipher, to use other codes and ciphers, to draw information from prisoners of war, and to interpret and communicate information. Elsewhere the nation's war machine was at last running at full tilt. Already the vanguard of Americans had been in France a year. The Texans were soon on their way.

Madison missed seeing his mother who went to New York to say good-by. He wrote her that it was the biggest disappointment of his life that he didn't see her. Death might be dancing on the horizon. About the transport ship he wrote her this description:

> We are certainly lucky in the transport proposition, for we are loaded on the best one there is [S.S. *Olympic*]. It is a former ocean liner and fixed up accordingly. Some of the staterooms are beautiful and all of them are well-equipped. . . . All the stained-glass and French windows have been painted black so that no light will be visible from the outside at night. . . . The magnificent ballroom and private dining rooms have been converted into gun and ammunition store houses.

Lt. Cooper put on his Sam Browne belt for the first time and said he felt "very European." This port of embarkation letter to Matoota (formerly Mama) ended:

> Well, dear, we are pulling away from the dock slowly. I am glad to go and only hope thereby to do some real good whether in the intelligence work to which Capt. Hatchitt says I am to be recalled, or in the infantry. They can decide where they want me and I'll do all I can. . . . Above all (you and the rest of my family) be cheerful and take things as they come.

The U.S. harbor letter was the only gloomy missive from Lt. Cooper of the AEF. When he reached the other side, he appeared bursting with good feeling. The transport put ashore at Le Havre, he wrote, ". . . in the prescribed manner and everything went off as planned. Practically none of our troops was seasick, which shows

that good health and exercise has a lot to do with it." Then as always
he was concerned for his mother's peace of mind. He cabled her of
his safe arrival, but soundly rapped the cost of the telegram in a
letter he wrote soon afterwards.

Bay-sur-Aube, an early destination, was his platoon's billet as
military gears meshed elsewhere preparing for the second battle of
the Marne. Lt. Cooper, billeting officer in Bay-sur-Aube, had trouble.
He had no interpreter. Somehow with the help of a meager seven
lessons in French taught at Camp Travis in Texas he got by as town
major. He gave his family a superficial account to prove he was on
top of his job:

> I have a fine place to stay with an old couple in a new cottage. . . .
> The rich man of this village is almost exactly like Pop except his
> language is some different. He and I get along fine. . . . There is only
> one girl at all attractive here. She is the daughter of a French major
> who sent his family out of Paris to escape the German air raids. All
> the other inhabitants are the ordinary run of old, old men and women
> and loads of cute kids with the most contented faces. The old people,
> like France, realize what war is; the children are more like America.

After a period of boredom that followed, life sweetened a bit
when the first shipment of U.S. mail arrived in Bay-sur-Aube. The
cool skeptic warmed up in a letter home when he wrote, "Christmas
hasn't a thing on today. The major brought us in an hour earlier
from drill and I found eight letters awaiting me. I haven't been as
happy in centuries. . . . Just realize that I would not be anywhere
else for anything under the present circumstances, and that all will
come out well, I know."

Always a close observer of the Waco scene, Cooper liked to
gossip. Being across the Atlantic barely slowed him down. He would
write to his mother, "If I am not mistaken, ———— was sup-
posed to be about to marry the old man once before. I can't understand how she missed out on all the officers at Camp MacArthur
[near Waco]. Surely she had some out there lined up."

Preparations for the September St. Mihiel salient were soon under
way. Lt. Cooper was at last in the midstream of infantry battle
preparation—then he was called to the army intelligence school in
Langres. It meant leaving behind Frenchmen he liked and Texans,
including Waco men, he was used to. He was not happy to leave
his platoon, which he claimed he had worked into a "plum good one."

Later he rejoined his 360th Infantry as assistant intelligence officer as the St. Mihiel push got started. Heavy artillery fire at 1 A.M. September 12 turned into a rolling barrage preceding a French tank advance at 5 A.M. Engineer detachments equipped with wire cutters and Bangalore torpedoes cleared the way for six American divisions. The advance was easier than the American command had expected. All initial objectives were taken on schedule. As the push proceeded, the Americans gained confidence and the First Army knew it was effective in tough fighting. The Texans, including Cooper, were in the battle breaking through mazes of wire and entrenchments called the quart-en-réserve and western end of the Bois le Pretre to the Moselle River. Here they remained until October 9–10 when they proceeded to the Meuse-Argonne front, and Cooper would relish the battle:

> You must have heard by this time that the 360th played a wonderful part in the first large scale American offensive. It was wonderful and I wouldn't be anywhere else for anything that could be offered me. . . . I wish I could tell you about the drive, but that will have to wait. . . . I sent you a telegram yesterday and hope it will go through without any hitches so as to allay your fears that I may have been brutally murdered in the conflict.

It was another note of manly swagger to silence an anxious family. Another letter home told of riding around the country spreading éclat.

German prisoners trudging in from the scorched, pocked earth of the western front began bringing the rumor of an impending German retreat. Soon the famed 11-11-11. Lt. Cooper tells what he saw November 11, 1918 at 11 A.M.:

> Today has been a wonderful day! I was up at the front riding around in the Cadillac sedan with a major from GHQ at the time the hostilities ceased (11 A.M.). The joy of the men was wonderful to see. Promptly on time the Germans left their front trenches in full view and went back toward the town laughing and yelling—all afternoon they sent up flares, rockets, and other fireworks.

Then Germans came visiting in bunches looking for white bread; liberated Allied prisoners came through his area in what he described as "hilarious droves." Liberated U.S. prisoners returned "and are having the time of their lives regaling the others with impossible narratives. They do not confirm the many atrocities of the Germans against prisoners," he said in a letter home.

His last France post was Heudicourt, a badly shelled and muddy village, located between the Meuse and Moselle Rivers near Mont Sec. He complained and disapproved, but finally got his mind on duties as an athletic and amusements officer. "Everyone realizes the problem of keeping the morale of the troops up during these trying times of inactivity." He was with a division of Pennsylvanians now—the 28th.

His immediate superior commended his energy, enthusiasm, and problem-solving ability. He said Cooper always made good. Again, success. He had prevailed at Camp Leon Springs when nearly half of his fellow officer trainees washed out. Now he tried his energy-intelligence quotient in army life and saw it excel among adults as it had excelled in high school and college.

The U.S.S. *Finland* carrying 2,480 men and 112 officers from Bordeaux, among them Madison Cooper, Jr., landed at New York City, May 1, 1919. Promoted to captain now, he received a fourteen-day leave and orders to report at his own expense to Camp Travis for discharge. His 28th Division could go to Philadelphia, and pass in parade before Independence Hall. Capt. Cooper passed up the parade; he was homesick and headed for Waco.

IV Ten Years

in Family Business

THE FAMILY WELCOMED its handsome hero home with a victory dinner, and when his luggage arrived, he had it taken to his old suite on the second floor of 1801 Austin Avenue. These three rooms under the towering cupola had been designed originally for Madison's use by architect Allen in 1905, and in 1919 he renewed his claim to them, this time permanently. Madison Cooper had thought the army might be the life for him, but with encouragement from his parents, a business career in Waco won out.

Everyone believed he would succeed his father to the presidency of the Cooper Grocery Company. M. A. Cooper had encouraged such a course with a sizable chunk of Cooper stock as a gift to his son. He also brought Madison along into the new decade with cash gifts to draw interest, turned notes over to him to initiate Madison into the loan business, and encouraged him to invest in Texas municipal and county bonds by giving him a portfolio of such securities.

Immediately after he left the army, Madison Cooper's days were filled with chores of a "made" job at the highly profitable Cooper Company and his nights and weekends were filled with parties and movies, much as they had been when he left home in 1917. The fact that there was no visible need for a manager of the confectionary-produce department at the Cooper Company must have been apparent early. But he stuck it out, because he didn't want to let his parents down, and he had to keep busy.

Courses in English he took 1911-1915 at the University of Texas soon asserted their grip on his imagination. College and steady reading taught him to admire the work of writers. Wishing to emulate them, he tried again to set his own thoughts on paper. He taught himself touch typing. At first he worked in his bedroom with the door closed, but eventually, a garret office appealed to him and he turned his thoughts toward the Cooper attic then used only for storage.

Madison selected a long, narrow room with one casement window under the east gable of the house. It was just right for a one-man work space: big enough for a file cabinet and trunk storage, several tables and a desk, a bookcase, and chairs—and small enough for privacy. The little room would be too crowded for visitors to spend much time there. Its location sealed him off from everyone admirably. There were just two ways to reach the little office: up a winding stairway from the back door, or from the second floor bedroom hall. He set up files to hold every scrap of paper which might be useful to him in writing and in dealing with other people—letters, records, memoranda, receipts, notes he jotted down about himself and others. He even kept a growing collection of letters from women.

Off-limits to everyone, the little office symbolized a turning point in his life. At the age of twenty-eight, in 1922, he chose this room to grapple with the problems of his life. Things weren't going as he had hoped, with young women or work. He was either going to have to change, or effect change in his surroundings. There appeared to be no chance to put new methods to work at the Cooper Company as long as his father was president, and he tasted his first defeat with a girl he loved this year.[1] So he met his frustration on paper. He started grinding out a book on a subject so impossible for him to handle it was bound to fail: he would write a philosophical tome describing how to solve social problems and resolve national issues. Meager experience with writing had proved how hard it was to sit still at the typewriter, but Madison Cooper gritted his teeth and went to work. He forced himself to sit in a hard, straight-backed chair two hours daily and type. Months of this enforced labor eased the difficulty of writing and he was able to work eagerly during all of his free time.

And so, during the first years following World War I, Madison Cooper, Jr., took still another step toward withdrawal from his contemporaries in Waco. Not that he ceased to enjoy travel and parties from time to time. He taught some of his friends to play mah-jongg and he kept up the dating, with the bright girls getting the first calls. He refused to confide their names to his mother. If Mrs. Cooper were to inquire about his date for the evening, his quick answer was "Katrinka Schultz" or "Hermione Smith," fictitious ploys to end the questions.

The Madison Cooper that Leland McCullough remembers from these years was an articulate man, a good mixer. Leland admired his wit, and observed that Cooper could talk as easily with children as with old people. C. H. Bell was a boy next door to the Coopers, and he, too, admired the tall young man in the big house on the corner.

> Mother always thought you were the true type of a rich young man—
> not spoiled—just to the manor born. Mother always insisted it was not
> "to the manner born" but "manor."
>   . . . As well as I can remember, you and I had only one conversation
> in our lives—I was trying like hell to make the grass on our lawn look
> as nice as your [man] made yours look by cutting a little trough
> between sidewalk and lawn—you came out and assured me the trouble
> was I was trying too hard. You were very nice about it.[2]

In 1924 Madison took his first cautious steps into philanthropy with a $50.00 gift to the Waco Community Chest. It was the first of annual gifts that grew much larger. For a while the First Presbyterian Church received his biggest gifts, several hundred dollars. The University of Texas was a close second.

At $2,400 per annum, his Cooper Company salary gives no indication that he was in a position to make substantial contributions to anyone. But his total income was seven to eight times larger and lent credence to his repeated statements that his first interest was *business,* meaning making money. Close behind it was what he came privately to hope would emerge as his real career—professional writing.

Gradually it had become easier to tap out his ideas on the typewriter. The philosophical book he produced ended up in a garbage can on West Forty-sixth Street in New York City after an agent told him it would never sell. No one else would ever have known he wrote it, if he hadn't admitted it nearly thirty years later. He called it three hundred thousand words of "non-fiction of the so-called 'panacea school' . . . [But the time was not wasted] As a matter of literary discipline, learning to stay put long enough to get a book on paper . . . the training was INVALUABLE."[3] Having failed with the book, the only way he knew to become a professional writer was to keep writing until someone recognized his worth. Believing this, he bore down on short stories, which he signed "Matt Cooper." It was hard work and he was producing them by the dozens, and by 1926 he had sold some of them. He earned only $360, a petty contribution to his hefty annual income that year—about fourteen thousand dollars. For some time he had cherished a hope to resign from his job at the wholesale grocery house when he became established as a writer. But sales trickled to nothing.

As his writing career sagged, his father for the first and only time publicly acknowledged that Madison was not interested in succeeding to the company presidency. M. A. Cooper sold his controlling interest in the Cooper Grocery Company to subordinates. For forty-seven years he had successfully directed his company, but now he knew it was time to let the younger men carry the load. He retained the title of president, however, and about 10 percent of the stock, but he put his increased capital into an active loan business.

At home M. A. Cooper brightened his wife's days by joining the First Presbyterian Church, and they marked the happy occasion by giving the Rev. Mr. Caldwell funds for a trip to the Holy Land. A stained-glass window at the church now memorialized the short life of little Christine.

Madison Cooper continued working at the Cooper Company as secretary of the board of directors, and as a salaried employee in Ed Barrett's grocery merchandizing department. He sat at a roll-top desk and his co-workers were convinced his "made" work bored him. Several days each week he bolted from his desk fifteen minutes early to get to one of the local movie houses before matinee prices changed.

When Madison wasn't working, he was busy with his countless activities including tennis or swimming (he learned to swim one summer in California) or hiking or working out at the YMCA. Not only the touch-and-go health of his childhood, but especially the U.S. Army had taught him to take good care of himself. It meant regular exercises and plenty of good food. If his weight slipped down, he found ways to get it back up to one hundred and seventy-five pounds.

A long-lived hatred of ignorance led Madison to seek out capable young men who needed to borrow money to attend college. He had money to lend to the right young fellow, he said. In truth, he had as much free advice on how to succeed at college as he had money. His loans to "deserving young people" were the only kind he liked to make. If he held notes from other people, they were gifts from his father, who transferred the paper to his son. M. A. Cooper considered his son Madison a good repository. He was careful with his money and increased it methodically.

Madison's distaste for ignorance coupled with a mounting disregard for the feelings of others led him to appoint himself keeper of good grammar among his contemporaries. It often stung them so hard they never forgave him, remembering the rest of their lives that he rapped their use of the past tense, or their stress on the wrong syllable—and he never seemed to care that they were cut.

The girls of his young manhood were now married and raising families. In 1927, at the age of thirty-three Cooper dated younger girls whom he thought were silly, and he told them so, but he wanted their company: because he was handsome and rich, he could get by with such tactlessness. Even though he proposed marriage sometimes, his offers were made with all the finesse of a freight train at full throttle. Since by his own admission he preferred beautiful girls from good families, he was asking for defeat. They didn't have to marry a martinet who wouldn't spend money on them and who demanded so much time to himself. It is safe to say he was willing to make a matrimonial alliance on his own terms, but he lacked the warm give-and-take an engagement to marry requires.

Madison A. Cooper, Jr., lost a few hundred dollars on a shoe and trunk factory in 1927, but other dividends and interest kept his income high. He seriously thought about the role of a gentleman farmer, but told no one. He only asked circumspect questions and listened to plans to bring a milk processing plant to Waco. His conduct emphatically reiterated his old edict: what I do is my business, not yours.

Doubtless one of the main reasons for his moody silence was disappointment over the fact that his short stories would not sell. Manuscripts which no one in Waco knew existed were stored in the attic at 1801 Austin Avenue as he temporarily gave up the dream of becoming a writer.

Curiosity about Madison Cooper's secretive activities spread from his friends to the general public. They began noting he was a mystery man, and imagined worse things.

But mystery does not begin to describe his family's reaction when he said good-by to the Cooper Grocery Company in 1929 to become, of all things, a dairyman! If they had suspected he was not what they considered a businessman, they knew it now. The new milk processing plant providing a market for raw milk was hardly an excuse for this sharp turn in his life's events.

He mimeographed a letter to all his co-workers expressing "appre-

ciation for the many contacts I have had through the Company."
The letter began:

> For some months now it has become increasingly apparent that if
> business interests I have outside of the Cooper Grocery Company are
> to develop as I want them to, I must have more time to devote to
> them. . . . The Cooper Grocery Company is so organized that it can
> easily adjust itself to take care of my duties, whereas my other interests
> are not. . . . I shall still live in Waco.[4]

Madison went into debt to buy a 1,440-acre bottomland farm
on the east bank of the Brazos River south of Waco. The sale was
consummated on January 2, 1930 at a price of $65,000 to be repaid
in yearly installments of $6,500, plus interest, for ten years. He
called the dairy operation Cooper-Taylor Herd, a label combining
the names of the financial backer and the experienced manager.

Continuing his search for new investment frontiers, he bought stock
in a bank at Eastland, in West Texas. The bank failed and cost him
money. The dairy business proved to be hard work and was so
unprofitable that it was a clear disappointment.

The national economic depression of the 1930s guided Madison
Cooper around another of his life's sharp turns. Combined with the
uncertainty of what to do next, the depression made him unhappier
than he realized. He refused invitations to parties in Waco, and virtually completed withdrawal from friendly contact outside the family
circle, except for escorting women to movies.

Madison, born with the privileges of wealth, already had what
others spend years seeking. Confronted with the peculiarly difficult
problem of building a useful life on the golden foundation provided
by his father, he had too much energy and intelligence, too much
pride, to spend his time on shallow conformities. Having no wife or
children to please, he must build his future life alone.

V The 1930s:

Experiment in Life

IN 1931 MADISON Cooper, Sr., was injured in an automobile accident, causing him to walk with a cane the rest of his life. And Mrs. Cooper's eyesight was fading because of cataracts.

Mrs. Cooper bought her shroud, and a new servant in the household, Mrs. Bertha Lee Walton, listened wide-eyed as Mrs. Cooper told her family that when her time should come, she wanted no embalming after death (Bertha believed she "didn't want them undertakers messing with her body"); that she wanted the coffin to stay closed during the funeral service ("she didn't want people saying how well she looked in death or what a good job the undertakers had done"); that she wanted her body taken from her home directly to the First Presbyterian Church, then to the cemetery where it was to be placed in a grave next to little Christine who had died in 1894. Mrs. Cooper exacted a pledge from her son Madison that her wishes would be carried out.

M. A. Cooper, Sr., continued a practice of many years—giving his property in equal portions to his daughter and son. In 1931 they received a block of interest-bearing notes on loans he had made. In the same way he gave them joint title to over thirty pieces of commercial and residential real estate in Waco and Temple, and a few farms. Lucile Cooper Lacy's children received small shares of a few of these properties. Mrs. Lacy's husband then learned it was hard if not impossible to do business jointly with Madison whose take-it-or-leave-it stance with prospective renters of the jointly owned property several times resulted in vacancies instead of reduced-rate income. Madison disliked negotiating over rents.

Probably his disinterest was heightened by the success he seemed to be having with his Columbia University home study courses in composition and short-story writing. His instructors in the early 1930s were Edward Hodnett, later chairman of the department of English at Ohio University, and Mack Gorham. Hodnett watched the short-story student get mired repeatedly in complex, but interesting, explanations and he suggested that Madison Cooper try a novel.

Many years later Hodnett recalled Cooper, the still-struggling short-story writer:

> My recollection of his writing is that, like that of Theodore Dreiser
> and other American naturalistic writers, it showed sociological dis-
> tinction rather than literary. Mr. Cooper had a great sense of fact—a
> keen awareness of the richness of the human drama. . . . In addition,
> he made up for what, in my perhaps fallible judgment, I would con-
> sider a lack of natural literary talent by an extraordinary diligence
> and tenacity.[1]

Unready for the novel suggested by Hodnett, Cooper turned to another Columbia teacher—Mack Gorham. Gorham's patience with
Cooper's faults as a writer and his steady encouragement led Cooper
to sign up for the same course twice. Cooper remembered these
two teachers nearly twenty years later.

> Had I not taken three correspondence courses at Columbia University
> (courses later discontinued because some official felt they were "not
> in keeping with Columbia's standing"), I probably would have con-
> tinued to write strictly from formula. . . . Columbia dis-converted me.
> Naturally, I am grateful to my teachers, Edward Hodnett, now of
> Athens, Ohio, and Mack Gorham, now of *Esquire's* advertising re-
> search. At no time did either tell me what to write, but they told me,
> and correctly in every instance, what I did well and what I did badly.[2]

He kept up his connections with New York City friends by continuing the annual excursions east. Among the people he met in
theater and literary work was Boyden Sparkes, former newsman and
writer for *Saturday Evening Post*. Sparkes was then in the early
stages of a successful career as a collaborator on autobiographical
books.[3] Sparkes opened doors for Cooper to literary circles and
clubs, and he obliged the Texan by keeping the secret of Madison
Cooper's writings. Later Boyden Sparkes wrote to Madison Cooper,
"But now [after publication of Cooper's first novel], I think, I
understand why you were reluctant even horrified at the thought of
Waco discovering you were writing short stories. The fate of the
Iconoclast . . . [William Cowper Brann] must have been haunting
you."[4]

Although he is reported to have been unpleasant at home, Cooper
the visitor was different in the memory of New Yorkers. Mack Gorham described him like this:

[Madison Cooper] was at home . . . and could relate to persons in New York City as far as Mrs. Gorham and I were aware. We found him a thoughtful and appreciative friend.

He was most tactful in remembering any little thing we might do for him—such as a special salad—and would recall it appreciatively on later occasions.

His wit was sometimes biting but inclined to be detached and objective. We never found him in any way personally sarcastic or malicious. He was a kind, good friend, a demanding person not only of others but himself as well.[5]

In the autumn of 1936 Mack Gorham of Columbia University found himself out of work as Columbia curtailed its home study department. Gorham and Cooper decided to gamble on one another; they would attempt to break into the documentary film field and into publishing together. Cooper would supply the material and Gorham would work out scenarios. Gorham would do research in New York City libraries when necessary, and he would act as agent for Cooper's stories and a proposed syndicated newspaper column. Cooper supplied Gorham with his living expenses during these joint ventures and Gorham signed notes for the money.

In late 1937 Madison Cooper got a batch of his short stories back from a New York author's agent and read in the rejection letter, "I certainly didn't mean to say you couldn't write. I think you have a very great ability in characterization, in the construction of new situations and in presenting a phase of life that heretofore has not been written about." She said he had personality in his thoughts, but they were then "so tame and so damn drab" that he would have to get more color out of life.

His response two weeks later boiled. "Allow me to thank you again for your efforts on my behalf. Too, please express my appreciation to your reader (unnamed) whose criticism of my work you forwarded to me." He slapped at the agent verbally, "Some day, perhaps, I can send you something you will find suitable to your clientele, but I promise it won't be any time soon."[6]

The bold rejection of the short stories added persuasively to Edward Hodnett's suggestion that Madison Cooper should attempt a novel. The short-story writer, after all, was acutely limited to a single incident and a handful of characters at the most. Cooper knew he liked reaching deeper into life, as a novel would require; yet he had wrestled so long with short stories that he was slow to give up the fight.

Meanwhile, taking infinite pains over his choices of investments, Madison Cooper put his Texas money to work elsewhere. And in 1937 he deposited in his Waco accounts the first profits from investment through the major stock exchanges. That year's income included $8,819 from such securities as AT&T, Massachusetts Investment Trust, Phillips Petroleum, Chrysler, Sears Roebuck, General Motors, and Standard Oil of New Jersey.

As the dividends from investments came in 1937 and 1938, he expanded his charitable gifts in Waco from the longstanding annual contributions to the Waco Community Chest and the First Presbyterian Church to include Baylor University and the Waco Chamber of Commerce. The last contribution was the first concrete evidence that Madison Cooper was willing to assume his obligation to help pull Waco out of the economic doldrums it had experienced with the decline in blackland cotton production and the depression of the 1930s. However, his contributions to the Waco Chamber of Commerce were interrupted after two years when the board of directors took Madison Cooper's financial support to mean that he was personally interested in working with them. Without seeking his agreement to his nomination, the chamber elected Madison to its board of directors. When he learned he was elected, he turned the job down without explanation. At the same time he made the first of a long list of personal and anonymous gifts to help the people of Waco in the only way he could work—"alone and unaided." In 1938 he provided $3,000 to help the Waco Public Library set up its Wheatley branch for Negroes living near the river. The same year he contributed to fund drives of Baylor University, his own Presbyterian church, and the National Jewish Appeal.

A turning point in Cooper history came on February 12, 1938, when old M. A. Cooper, Sr., relinquished the presidency of the wholesale merchandising company which he had founded and actively managed for sixty years. He took the title, chairman of the board, while Henry W. Carver, treasurer of the company since 1907, became president of the Cooper Company, Incorporated. An even more decisive turning point followed in short order. On April 30, 1938, Mr. Carver died and J. R. Milam, a vice-president of the company since 1907, was elevated to the presidency. E. C. Barrett, who had been Mr. Cooper's vice-president from 1897, continued as vice-president. This set the stage for the internal fireworks that helped bring an end to the Cooper Company more than a decade later.

Madison Cooper, Jr., continued as secretary of the company board for another ten years after his father relinquished the presidency, but during that time he took no active part in the management.

M. A. Cooper the board chairman set up a $100,000 trust fund for his son who vowed he would never spend the money. The son this year retained a lawyer, Hilton E. Howell. And about the same time he finished working out a complete timetable and itinerary for a 1939 trip he proposed to give his sister's four children, now grown or in their late teen years. They were to go to Europe together and visit places chosen by Madison. As it turned out, the Lacy children declined the offer through their parents, who didn't like the idea of all four of them on board ship the same time when war appeared imminent in Europe.

A chance encounter showing Madison Cooper's occasional effort at charm, a build-up which he later called one of his better efforts, came about this time. Miss Mary Lou Curry, then a student at Baylor University, was seated in Waco Hall for a performance of Ted Shawn and his dancers when a man whom she considered good-looking took the seat behind her. A pair of opera glasses belonging to a third person brought them together. They took turns watching the dancers through the glasses.

In the course of their conversation, the gentleman (Madison Cooper) suggested that Miss Curry read the biographies of Pavlova and Nijinsky, and somehow he got around to saying he had to stop to figure out every line of Browning. "That's not poetry, that's arithmetic," he told her.

He walked with her back to the dormitory, Burleson Hall, and as he was leaving, told her his name was Matt Cooper. He asked her if she lived at the front of the dorm, and if she put on shadow shows. She did not, but took no offense and he departed.

Several weeks later he telephoned her for a date, but she turned him down. Looking through the telephone directory, she confirmed there was no Matt or Matthew Cooper listed. She decided he was a traveling salesman who had hit town again.[7]

Madison continued to spend hours daily in the third floor office at the Cooper home writing and rewriting another short story called "The Catch of Sironia." The principal character of the story was Launcelot Thaxton. Poor Lance was mentally deficient and was highborn—the son of banker Calvin Thaxton and his wife Millicent, both descendants of so-called Old South aristocracy in a town Cooper named Sironia.

He was feeling his way, consciously or not, toward the novel and was polishing the skill of characterization.

The story substance of "The Catch of Sironia" resulted in mentally deficient Lance finding his own happiness without the long-time meddling help of his mother, Miss Milly. And even though she had tried to marry him off to several girls among Sironia's best young womanhood, he managed to remain single.

When the editors of *The Amateur Writer*[8] chose "The Catch of Sironia" for publication in a 1939 issue, Cooper's pride glowed, although the short story earned only $12 for him.

Old Mrs. Cooper's eye ailment demanded the attention of a surgeon in 1938. The cataracts were removed in a hospital in Dallas. Recuperating at home, she seemed to have lost the strength to overcome the effects of the operation. She grew weaker slowly. She was seventy-seven years old. At 6:30 P.M. on Friday, March 24, 1939, she died.

There was no need for discussion of funeral arrangements, since Mrs. Cooper had told her children eight years before what she wanted done.

In the Coopers' fading fleur-de-lis parlor the casket was placed. It was the finest Bertha Walton, the family cook, had ever seen. She said it was tufted so deeply "You could hide your hands in the folds."

Only the family saw the corpse and the coffin was closed forever. Burial on Saturday was at the family plot at Oakwood Cemetery in Waco where a marble angel still dominates the scene. At home the funeral flowers had perfumed the whole house with such a confusion of fragrance that Bertha could not forget the drama of death.

For months after the death of his wife, M. A. Cooper seemed tired. His mind was alert, he continued reading his favorite newspapers, but he sometimes sat at a window and stared through space for an hour at a time. All his property except a few old-issue stocks and his home were now the property of his children. A fall down the wide Austin Avenue steps at home had further incapacitated him and toward the end of April, 1940, he contracted pneumonia. He was over eighty-four years old when he died on April 24. His last wish was carried out: the funeral procession passed along South Fourth Street en route to Oakwood Cemetery in order to pass the wholesale grocery house he had founded.

Alone now in the big old house, Madison asked Bertha Walton if she would stay on and do his laundry and mending, besides cooking three meals a day. Her apartment over the Cooper garage was the only home she had known for many years. When she agreed he told her that he wanted flowers from the yard kept in the reception hall during the growing season to make the empty mansion less dismal. Especially were flowers to be near his mother's photograph on a table, and if there were no flowers available, greenery was to be used.

VI Matt Cooper Alone

MADISON, EVER CONSCIOUS of his unique position in his community, spent more time than ever in his attic office with a view of the William Waldo Cameron house across Eighteenth Street. That house would become the Waco Public Library in 1941. He had never bothered with what other people thought of him, and the deaths of his parents in 1939 and 1940 gave him the freedom to live his life exactly as he pleased. It pleased him to be different. At the same time it suited him to keep his life a secret from everyone. The result was a clutter of egocentricity resulting in eccentricity, much like his office.

In that office he had a kitchen timer which became celebrated locally. It was on his desk in the attic office with a jar of paste, ink, paperweights of unlikely design, and pigeonhole shelves holding pencils, small tools, and brushes. He used the kitchen timer to clock visits when he wanted to limit a visitor's stay and to measure his own time spent on chores. The disturbing ticks of the timer were enough to rattle the most confident visitor. He used it on himself to stay on the strict schedule comparable to the military discipline he learned in World War I. The timer bell pinged but once, an insignificant sound, one might think. But in case it seemed so to his visitor, Cooper would stand at the sound to emphasize that the interview was over.

Overhead in his office hung a fly swatter. It dangled inconveniently aside from the maze of light wires over his working areas. His desk was nothing more than a stocky, plain writing desk covered with heavy brown wrapping paper. The paper was held in place with gummed paper tape. His chair, a simple swivel style, had no arms. Its special characteristic was a homemade backrest. This was made of three magazines, folded once and wrapped in high quality damask table linen and stitched with coarse black thread. A complicated web of heavy white twine bound it to the chair. When the back rest slipped, Matt Cooper added a small cube of lead to balance its weight. He knew his office was junky, but it suited him, and he didn't countenance comments on its appearance.

Shining from above, according to need, were three sixty-watt electric light bulbs—two shaded, one bare. Each was suspended from its own cord at a carefully arranged angle. In its contorted drop from the ceiling, each was supported by an average of nine varieties of restraint on gravity. These were thin wires of three dimensions, ordinary package-wrapping string, paper clips, black gummed tape, rubber bands, insulated wire, and rubber tubing. One shaded bulb could be adjusted to shine into the face of a seated visitor.

In this office he read letters from Mack Gorham admitting they should give up their various unsuccessful joint projects. Gorham had found no cash market for Cooper's stories, nor had other ideas scored with publishers or film companies. Even so, Matt would not discredit the aid his old friend provided, for Gorham was the only source of criticism and encouragement that Cooper the writer had. Gorham had read and criticized many short stories and would continue to comply with Cooper's request to read his material from time to time.

In the attic office Matt Cooper in 1941 tapped out the first pages of a novel he had at last decided to attempt. The seed of the novel would be "The Catch of Sironia," the short story published in 1939. The major shift from short story to novel occurred when he expanded not only the number of characters in his story, but when he decided to etch in drama and detail to illustrate how sweet little children grow up to be shaped, not only by their heritage, but by their surroundings.

Early among the characters he drew from "The Catch of Sironia" was a boy, Roane Lea, originally named with two surnames from his mother's family. Roane Lea typified what Cooper thought was a normal, average boy—the kind people generally like, not a spectacular talent or unique personality. For the novel the author chose another name. It was Tammas Abercrombie Lipscomb. Solidifying this Tam in his mind, novelist Cooper described the character in a notebook: Tam would have reddish brown hair and brown eyes. As a boy he looked like one man Cooper knew; as an adult, another. Neither was Cooper kin. Tam's character, personality, and the events of his life evolved from the author's experience and the sweep of events in an imaginary town named Sironia. As he enlarged the scope of his medium, Cooper the fumbling writer became Cooper the magnetic storyteller. His work was a deliverance. He had accumulated emotions of a lifetime for which he had found no satisfactory outlet. His novel became a means for expressing the feelings he was reared to conceal. This is not to say, however, that he expressed his own history, or that of anyone else, when his feelings jelled in his characters. There would be bits and pieces of many living persons in the story.

As Cooper's tale unfolded, incidents in Tam's life came from stories the author had heard in Waco, Georgia, Tennessee, and North Carolina. He researched other facts from Waco newspapers of the period covered by the novel. Mostly his incidents grew out of the natural and logical sequence of the fictitious lives he shaped. He had short stories stored in the attic which he planned to exhume for use in the novel.

Here's how the forty-six-year-old author described Tammas Abercrombie Lipscomb, whose story this chiefly was:

> Very likable, very human, very weak where women are concerned. A good businessman, he means well toward everybody, but slips often. He is brave, even when his hotheadedness is not in charge. His love for Nelia (Cornelia Haydn in Sironia) is the only really beautiful thing in his life, it is separate from all else and stays that way. . . .
> Brought up to hate the ways of the snooty Old South, Tam finally comes to accept the Old South at its own valuation—as an adult would accept a child's dreams, which the adult would like to share but cannot. Tam and Bessie [Nelia's cousin whom Tam weds to prevent her marriage to poor Lance, as maneuvered by Miss Milly] suit perfectly.[1]

As the story proceeded in his mind, the author adopted the working title, *The Hills of Sironia.*

Sketching in the background for a big story of a small city, Cooper drew his plantation families back to pre-1800 beginnings. No Anglo-American plantations are known to have existed in Texas at this time. Certainly none grew into towns, then into cities, as did Sironia.

Cooper's town evolved in his mind to consist of three shallow hills supporting three mansions. Less important homes and the business section emerged in the area between the hills. The mansions were named Storrow, Thaxton, and Haydn manors. Storrow and Thaxton manors were modeled imaginatively after such Natchez, Mississippi, antebellum showplaces as Melrose, or Riverview on the Tombigbee River near Columbus, Mississippi. Overlooking the entire Sironian scene was the original plantation home, Syringa. It had similar double flight entrance stairs to those of Stanton Hall in

Natchez, the William Gibbs House in Charleston, and another such structure in Tuscaloosa, Alabama. Its observatory was a Jeffersonian dome. Haydn manor had once been like the Thaxton and Storrow residences, but it burned. It was replaced by a two-story frame residence with a cupola and Gothic revival ornamentation similar to Ed C. Barrett's home in Waco.

Back among the characters he took Ada Lea from "The Catch of Sironia" and rechristened her Moira Thorndyke Lipscomb. In the short story she had been a Lea store clerk whom Marshall Lea married on the rebound after being jilted by Miss Milly Thaxton. In *The Hills of Sironia* she became the Haydns' maid. When Marshall Lipscomb (originally Marshall Lea) married her, he still did so as an affront to Millicent Letitia Thaxton Thaxton. Cooper found himself writing into his novel the lives of many people who were often more real to him than living persons he knew.

Cooper dramatized his Sironians' existence, rather than generalizing in expository tones. He displayed in full detail the causes and results of the story development with description, dialogue, characters, and subcharacters interacting on one another's lives. He believed that other authors left out such details to get on with the story. Cooper put it all in, and the detail emerged as a triumph of his work. He was writing what he hoped would be a completely motivated romantic novel, the only one of its kind at the time. He found himself creating a life-size drama within the framework of a novel, and he swept his narrative along on incidents, thoughts, and conversations of his characters. Sometimes he would write as many as five thousand words of his story during a morning. During later revision he could cut perhaps four thousand to get the effect he wanted, but his method stayed consistent, clear.

Yet as the story of his novel boomed along, he found himself in trouble. He had scores of characters taking flesh and blood form. Drawing them into the context of their relationships not only with one another, he also cast them in relation to their ancestors and children. So to clear things up permanently, he worked up a genealogy chart for the "Hill families." It was kept for ready reference so he could check who was descended, for instance, from Sironia Reardon (for whom the town was named) and Pluto Haydn, and how Trina Storrow happened to be a distant cousin, therefore a suitable mate, for the wonderful wastrel Jed.

Cooper kept a notebook describing every one of his 83 characters. He was writing a book which demanded that the reader know the characters as well as he knew his best friends. On this depended much of what Cooper was trying to say. It was to be a book about human beings, many of the best, and a few of the worst. Neither biographical nor autobiographical, it was telling the story of a vanished era (1900–1921) in American social and business history. It was a period of sharply drawn, indefensibly overbearing social distinctions which, viewed in later perspective, Madison Cooper believed contributed to a finer, a more warming result than the social climate replacing it after World War I.

The town of Sironia became so important in the story that he compiled a map for his daily use. He needed to have at hand a diagram showing Aurelia Street, the road to Chalcedonia, and the relation of Reardon's Pasture to Syringa. Although a notable example of bad penmanship, his map of Sironia was essential. He attached it to a printed map of the United States hanging against his office wall. A Texas map was placed so as to drop down over Sironia's chart. Such was his practice before visitors came to see him. He discussed his novel writing with no one in Waco. Only Mack Gorham of New York City saw an occasional chapter.

The Hills of Sironia from the beginning was another of his many secret projects. He maintained two work tables in his office: one for business, one for writing. As appointment time neared, the timer pinged, he covered his typewriter, he pulled down the map of Texas, and turned his mind to other matters.

Other ideas born in the attic office included Madison Cooper's futile campaign to obtain a commission in the U.S. Army on his own terms. He made first inquiries in 1940, when at forty-six he was already past conscription age. He would have been exempt from the draft, due to his farming-dairying operation on the Brazos. Initial inquiries gave him no encouragement and his quick mind shelved the effort for a while. He came back to it soon, however, and saw recruiters in Texas cold-shoulder his requests for a rank higher than the captaincy he held in World War I. Admitting he was overaged, he let them know that he was fit. At Waco Army Flying School he passed the army physical examination and learned that his blood pressure was right for a man of twenty. He admitted his left knee troubled him during a recent trip to New York, but it never bothered him when he ran the mile three times a week at Waco Municipal Stadium. This was only part of his regular gym work. Standing straight at six feet and one-half inches, he still weighed a healthy one hundred and seventy-five pounds.

The U.S. Army's cool treatment inspired a paper vendetta by Matt Cooper against U.S. Army policy. It began in 1942 and lasted a year through a prolonged barrage of letters. One of the earlier thrusts to get back into the army went to the adjutant general at the War Department in Washington, D.C.:

> For almost eighteen months I have tried, here, [in Waco] and in San Antonio, to get the right answer to one question: Is there a *need* by the army for former World War I officers, out of touch with the military for a long time, to return to active duty?
>
> Most of these high-ranking (active) officers with whom I have talked—several times—state frankly and I am sure, sincerely, although not in the words I use: That the army does not need such former officers, nor does the army want them; that due to political pressure, such officers can get themselves back in service, i.e., if they cannot be eliminated by physical examination.[2]

Cooper concluded this thrust with a four and one-half page autobiography, typed and single spaced, emphasizing details of his World War I activity. He was convinced that he should be commissioned a lieutenant colonel, partly because he was now nearly fifty years old. He reasoned that had he stayed in the army after World War I, as he contended he wished to do, he would surely by 1942 have attained even a higher grade than lieutenant colonel. For this reason the army ought to recognize that as a man of means, a man willing to sacrifice his personal income for a much, much smaller salary in the U.S. Army, a man who had invested over 10 percent of his income in U.S. treasury bonds the preceding two years, a man capable by instinct and experience to handle administrative and management duties, that he, Madison Cooper, Jr., was actually making a concession by offering to reenter the army as a lieutenant colonel. He explained:

> I do not need a job, nor do I need more income than I already have (my 1941 income tax . . . paid on March 15th and the additional assessment due to changes in depreciation rates allowed, chiefly, totaled slightly more than $8,000.00).
>
> If taken from my work on war duty, my income will be reduced, perhaps considerably, and the tax on same will, also. This is mentioned

because, while I think in the right job I could make up for the loss
to the government; the government should think so, too.

. . . I do not mind the inconvenience, nor the financial loss, if I am
to be given a job . . . worth it, that is, a job which needs to be done,
and one I am confident I can do.

According to present laws, there is little or no likelihood of my being
"drafted" for any kind of service; but I do not want to use my "age
immunity" to avoid service if the kind for which I am fitted is available.
I have no immediate family, and, even if I could, would place no
restrictions on where I might be sent.

In short he considered this letter the ultimate rationale.

The army was unimpressed. It wasted no time in declining his
offer:

Due to the fact that you desire only to be considered for the rank of
lieutenant colonel, this office finds that you do not meet the specifica-
tions laid down by the War Department and therefore two copies of
your personal data sheet are returned. The file is closed.[3]

His correspondence was channeled early the next year, 1943, to
the commanding general of Camp Hood (later Fort Hood) located
near Killeen, Texas. This series of communications resulted in a
Texas recommendation for appointment as a major. Later the War
Department declined to award the commission, but in the interim
Cooper turned it down because the army would not give him ninety
days to get his affairs in order. He needed time to turn over management of city real estate, farm properties, and his securities to
trusted individuals.

Cooper in the spring made an attempt to get his military commission via the political route. He wrote his congressman, W. R.
Poage: "It is hoped you can find time to consider the present status
of my two-year effort to be recommissioned in the Army."[4] A two-
page condensation of the developments followed. Nothing resulted
beyond an exchange of pleasant letters.

While admitting that he was not commando material, Cooper
said he was in far better physical condition than the average civilian
his age. Throughout his entire paper siege he understood he could
go back into the army as a captain, but he was always reminded
that what he was doing as a civilian probably resulted in greater
aid to the war effort than a captain's duties.

Army efforts exhausted, this persistent civilian directed a parting plea at the U.S. Navy. He wrote only once, asking simply if there were any chance of getting into the navy with the rank comparable to major "for which I was recommended in the army." Turned down there also, he gave up.

VII Making Waco
a Better Place

DURING WORLD WAR II, as always, Madison Cooper was probably the least understood of well-established men. Somehow his values were different.

The only concept the general public in Waco had clearly in mind was that Madison Cooper was a strange one! Absolutely no one was so important as to throw Cooper off his rigid daily schedule of activity. Kind people said his rushed impatience was not to offend, but to get the most out of every day.

His lawyer, Hilton E. Howell, illustrated Madison Cooper like this: "He would call to say he wanted to see me at 1:30 in the afternoon to ask a couple of questions. He was never late. He either arrived exactly on time or a few minutes early, and he never stayed longer than the brief time he asked for. To be sure our time wasn't wasted, he took notes on what I said. If I later refuted any statements—in the smallest way—he set me straight."

At this time Madison Cooper never rode in an automobile when he had time to walk. If he walked, his pace was hurried. He took big steps; he rarely stopped to talk on the street—unless he knew an individual had information he wanted. During his business day there was no familiar give and take in conversation so widely practiced and admired in Texas. For years during his work week he appeared in the same dark sweater with leather-patched elbows. His shoes were repaired over and over until they would no longer take repair. And the public, knowing he was a wealthy man, considered him a spectacle in poor man's clothing.

At church, however, and on evenings out when meeting with out-of-town people, Madison Cooper dressed well, in business suits and starched shirts. He consistently sat at the rear of the church pews in a folding chair, one of several placed there to expand seating room. Before the church installed its air conditioning, Madison Cooper brought his own cooling device with him in hot weather—an improvised fan made from a cardboard pencil tablet back. He never waited for the benediction or to shake the pastor's hand but left immediately at the end of the sermon.

At home during the week he answered the telephone in his third floor office during three hours—from eight until eleven in the morning. He ignored other calls when he was busy.

What most of his fellow-citizens didn't know in these years was his generosity to a large number of good causes. In 1943 alone he made cash contributions to the First Presbyterian Church, Blackland Army Air Field library, American Red Cross, Waco Public Library, Waco YMCA, McLennan County (for county probation officer's work fund), United Jewish Appeal, Waco Chamber of Commerce, Tulip (Arkansas) Cemetery Fund, Waco Community Chest, the Waco annex of McCloskey Hospital in Temple, and the City of Waco for a fund to convert Mackey Park into a park for Negroes. It became Bledsoe-Miller Park. As usual, his Community Chest gift was highest. Every solicitor for these causes agreed to keep his gift confidential. Since his gifts were anonymous, hearsay indicted him as tight-fisted and selfish, and he deliberately cultivated this image.[1]

Because he made no local disclosure of his earlier short-story writing and work on his novel, and because he discussed his stock market investments with no one except his investment counselors and the Internal Revenue Bureau, he was actually believed to be idling away his time in some unknown, perhaps useless pursuit at home. Some people, curious about their neighbor, imagined he was deciphering secret codes such as he had done twenty-five years earlier in the U.S. Army intelligence service. Even the several women he dated knew very little about his life.

Among his secretly growing capabilities was composition of his own lease contracts and other legal agreements. The older he grew, the better and tighter leases he could draw up. As he approached fifty, his mind was exquisitely exact. It ranged the scale of alternatives and weighed advantages with delicacy and precision. He cut through the underbrush of detail and distraction, as he did in 1943 when he composed a long, written instrument of another kind.

Having by nature long assessed his life, his fortune, the future, the past, and the present, he drew up with only occasional counseling with his attorney[2] an irrevocable and perpetual trust dated September 1, 1943. As a memorial to his parents, he entitled the trust the Madison Alexander Cooper and Martha Roane Cooper Foundation. He wanted it called the Cooper Foundation and it was to be known for its work, contrary to the anonymity he sought for his "personal" gifts. Net income from the trust was to be used "for any charitable, educational, or benevolent purpose which in the opinion of the trustees will make Waco, Texas, a better or more desirable city in which to live."

Cooper summoned to the office of J. R. Milam, president of the Cooper Company, the trustees of his choice to divulge the news and nature of his foundation while asking them to form the original board. Besides Milam they were Edward C. Barrett, a long-time bachelor friend of both Madison and his father and one of three founders of the Cooper Company; Edward Y. (Ned) Boynton, attorney; Raymond B. Goddard, businessman, University of Texas alumnus, and member of Cooper's college business fraternity; Hilton E. Howell, Cooper's lawyer and the fourth University of Texas graduate on the board; and U. Calvert Sterquell, another Cooper Company officer. They heard Madison Cooper read the long, inclusive indenture.

For such an ambitious objective, the Cooper Foundation had a small total worth: $25,000. That beginning sum left the trustees wondering how they could carry out the sweeping purpose of the trust. Could they possibly make Waco, Texas, a better and more desirable place for living with the modest income resulting out of only $25,000 in U.S. treasury bonds drawing 2½ percent interest? Cooper said he soon would add another $25,000 in bonds and would supply $500 to defray administrative expenses. Yet if the foundation were to achieve even modest aims, the trustees had to believe in the unseen. Certainly the occasion excited more questions than answers.

He asked them to submit one suggestion each within thirty days of the very first meeting. Each trustee then agreed to come back the next April to an annual meeting with five ideas for good use of foundation income.[3]

The first annual meeting took place as planned on April 26, 1944, in the home of the chairman of the board at 1801 Austin Avenue. Although the permanent endowment fund stood at $50,000, still drawing only 2½ percent ($1,250) a year, the trustees supported foundation goals with their presence. This time they could only discuss possible projects. The trustees agreed to investigate the feasibility of four suggestions: instituting a musical program for the city, locating an art gallery in Waco, furthering visual education on both the public school and adult levels, and establishing a natural amphitheater. Nothing, as it turned out, came of these ideas at the time.

These early days of the foundation show Madison Cooper's continued contributions to "the war effort." Not only were his farms producing food and fiber, not only was he investing a large share of his considerable earnings in U.S. treasury bonds, but also he had a personal USO operation at home, the Victorian mansion he acquired in a family trade with his sister after their father died.

Lieutenants stationed near Waco had ready access to his home on Sunday afternoons. He wrote many of them that they could find sanctuary there from such discomforts as the attentions of Waco's teenage girls "who can't seem to leave you alone" and from the Texas heat. He suggested they could use the place for a quick change of clothing or cleanup; to pass the time either by sitting on the lawn or porch and watching the cars go by; or they could go inside the house to read from his personal library. Further, they should consider his house a headquarters for telephone messages or appointments with fellow officers.

Far greater in scope was his hospitality to enlisted men. From early 1943 until the end of the war in 1945, Madison Cooper opened his home every Saturday to from four to six soldiers who came to eat home-cooked meals and spend the night at no cost to themselves. All were screened as "the better sort" by Mrs. T. B. Brazelton at the Waco USO where she then worked as a volunteer with many other Waco women.

Cooper's wish in this connection was to make life a bit pleasanter for the enlisted men who had little means for buying their own entertainment. Bertha Walton prepared six hundred and eighty meals, and was later cited for her "war work" by Camp Hood officials. There was nothing commonplace about Mrs. Walton's menus.

Typical fare for Saturday dinner included cream of tomato soup served with buttered croutons, scalloped turkey, buttered English peas, candied yams, congealed fruit salad, hot rolls (sometimes biscuits), iced tea and coffee, and crêpes suzette. Other evenings she served chicken chow mein, corn timbales, asparagus au gratin, glazed carrots, vegetable salad, butterhorns, angel food cake with whipped cream and pineapple, and iced tea and coffee. The food Mrs. Walton served the soldiers was characteristic of the dishes Madison Cooper liked. Eating good home-cooked food daily was the only domestic luxury he allowed himself. Wartime food rationing was a problem when she ran short on sugar and coffee. Otherwise Cooper had plenty of meat because he had his own steers and hogs butchered. Vegetables also were sent in from the farm. When the dishes were washed, Bertha still had work to do. She cleaned the bedrooms where the guests slept, cooked breakfast for them if they stayed that long, and laundered the sport shirts and pajamas their host lent them when needed. Often they came without knowing they would spend the night.

The end of the war in 1945 weakened Matt Cooper's determination to keep the dairy in operation. Labor and equipment problems likewise ate away at his resolve, and nine months after the war ended he decided Texas A&M in College Station needed his Brazos River farm more than he did. It would be the largest personal gift of his career. He deeded the dairy-hog-mule-horse-crop-cottonwood-pecan-poultry operation to A&M to be used as an experimental and demonstration farm, and as a memorial to Texas farmers of World War I and II. With inventory, the bottomland place assessed at $191,032.70.

Among the several aims he desired for the experimental and demonstration farm was that it should show dairying methods suitable to Central Texas. He emphasized that it should be run on practical and economical lines and that "all farmers (college trained or not) [should] feel free to come to said farm for advice about their problems and for inspection of farm practices suited to privately operated farms, both large and small." He repeated in the gift indenture that the ". . . farm will at all times be such as to cause the average Texas dirt farmer to feel welcome and want to come back for more information."

He wanted a marker at the entrance to read in part:

Central Texas Memorial Farm

As of February 1st, 1946, these approximately seventeen hundred acres of farmland, together with their improvements, implements, livestock and other equipment were donated as an operating dairy-farm by Madison A. Cooper, Junior, Waco, Texas, for perpetual ownership and management by the Agricultural and Mechanical College of Texas.

In April 1946 he divulged this arrangement to the foundation board, informing them that the farm would revert to Cooper Foundation if A&M "ceases to own it, ceases to operate it, borrows money on it, or fails to erect a marker specified in the indenture of the gift," a copy of which was placed in the foundation's safety deposit box at the bank.[4]

Shucking off the responsibilities of a time-consuming farm operation gave him more time than ever for his novel. Novel? It was now novels. The ambitious, completely motivated romantic story grew and grew. Characters he had created twenty-five years earlier tumbled about in a spectacular story. He held the language of the narrative in the vernacular, a level he believed would communicate with such faithful novel readers as himself. Never once did he dream the book would go into the hands of unfriendly readers, that is, people unaccustomed to the singular lives and loves of fictional human beings on the printed page. He meant for his characters to live through believable incidents as they grabbed the reader's imagination and touched every portion of his mind. The story was written honestly. To insure its integrity, he had cast it in a mold he understood—an early twenty years of his own life. Children, an important part of the whole, were imaginary young friends of the author.

Three years after the Cooper Foundation organizational meeting in 1943, the trustees put all big ideas aside to make the first gift from the fund. At a called meeting they approved foundation purchase of a $100 trailer for the Waco Fire Department. The trailer was used to haul a boat needed by the department's rescue squad when it set out on Waco's rivers, lake, or creeks, to drag for drowning victims.

When the foundation was five years old it regained the hapless dairy farm. Texas A&M relinquished it in favor of eighteen thousand acres it acquired in a twenty-five-year arrangement with the U.S. War Assets Administration. The new A&M farm site was near McGregor in the blacklands west of Waco where the Bluebonnet Ordnance Plant operated during World War II. The school put the large tract of land to work as an experiment center for research in beef cattle, sheep, goats, forages, grassland improvement, grain crops, soil fertility, cropping systems, weed and brush control, and cotton. Its name would be the Livestock and Forage Research Center, and in time, Texas A&M earned full title to six thousand three hundred and seventy-two acres. It was an indirect result of Madison Cooper's beneficence.

The Cooper property then was leased to an individual on a cash basis to operate as an agricultural enterprise—part of the assets of the Cooper Foundation.

VIII *Sironia Story Grows*

ALTHOUGH MADISON COOPER called on memories and news-paper back issues for some incidents in the novel, and although here and there are written his impressions of a few people he had known or heard about, the author could hardly put down so many words on humanity without revealing something of himself. He did so occasionally throughout the story, but nowhere more fully than in the Sironia character, Charles Cahoon Storrow. Storrow is de-scribed in the author's working notes as looking like three different men at three different periods in their lives. Before the story ended Cooper revised Charles's birthdate to August, 1895. This appears on a second age-chart. Originally, Cooper had Storrow being born in August, 1894—about the time the prematurely born author should have entered the world. Below the parallels proceed in the author's own words:

> Charles came ahead of time (an offense of which he was never again to be guilty) and weighed "practically nothing." He whined piteously and continuously at a world he obviously didn't like at all at the time— and not too much later. . . . Jed . . . had announced seriously . . . "What do you mean Cousin Carietta's little Charles is measly and doing poorly? I say he's doing doggone well to've been strained through cheesecloth—twice."[1]

> A beautiful child, [Charles like Madison Cooper] he was too well behaved, too subdued and too well-cared-for to be an attractive one.[2]

From the very first it is evident that, while a manly little fellow, Charles Storrow is not like other boys, "A gentleman before his time." When the boys play games at ten years of age he plays with them, excels, is liked but not looked up to, because he has too great a sense of property and right. Busy with his soldiering, books, and exercise.

Sironia's newspaper editor thinks about the boy Storrow:

59

What was it Charles lacked? Not looks. He was the handsomest speci-
men of youth-flesh Caleb had ever seen. Not intelligence: he led his
classes. Not strength: it was said he could best any boy in school "his
size" if he wanted to. (He never appeared to want to.)[3]

Charles Storrow contemplates himself at the age of nineteen:

Charles liked people—until the question of money or personal ad-
vantage came up. Then, somehow all the likeable qualities, all their
honest efforts to be agreeable seemed to stand out as so many weapons
to get what they were after. Was he saying people should be the way *he*
wanted them to be—instead of the way they were? Would he ever get
. . . "the right slant"?[4]

Charles Storrow working at the bank is much like the young
Cooper who for twelve years stayed with the wholesale grocery business, but never liked it.

Charles's natural independence was Madison Cooper's own: ". . .
it's *both* Mister Charles's strength and his weakness that he doesn't
give a damn about what others think of him so long as he thinks he's
right."[5]

This is not to say that the character Charles Storrow was fully
autobiographical. Far from it. As a youth Storrow disliked all routine, all work for money alone, all business procedure. Cooper all
his life worked best on a demanding schedule. He enjoyed earning
money on his own terms. Business procedure was a primary pleasure
of his life.[6]

Storrow was a violinist; Cooper was no kind of musician, nor did
he like symphony or opera. Unlike his creator, Storrow was poor
throughout his childhood and early manhood. Storrow was elected
to the U.S. Senate and Storrow got married. Before he decided
marriage was in order, Storrow kept a mulatto mistress—a fictional
ploy Cooper devised to get his reader off the scent of parallels between himself and the Sironia character. Both the author and his
character were World War I officers, but Cooper had no parade
and celebration to welcome him back to Waco as did Charles in
Sironia. Both were writers in their early manhood; Charles's work
was made to seem stilted and unnecessary—completely out of tune
with the times, and he kept it that way deliberately. Here the simi-
larities and easy contrasts end. Countless other circumstances and
incidents in Charles's life had no parallel in the author's. The character was only roughly similar to the author.

Cooper's Sironian women either stayed on the pedestal where all women belonged, or fell entirely from grace. A leading character, Millicent Letitia Thaxton Thaxton, voiced Cooper's fundamental attitude when she said:

> *"Our* [Sironian quality] men are apt to be that way." Miss Milly's tone was one of satisfied complacency rather than displeasure. "Very, very—human. They put their women on pedestals—"
> "—and then *see* that they stay there." [voice of Marshall Lipscomb] "Naturally." She approached smugness.[7]

Among several direct variations to such an attitude is the character Laurine Lane, a woman obviously admired by the author. "There was something rather—splendid," he wrote, "about a girl's preferring disgrace . . . to marrying the man she loved because he didn't want to marry her."[8] An interesting observation about Laurine when she ran away from Sironia to find no life awaiting her except prostitution. But we can be sure that when Cooper painted her into the story as an individual to admire, it resulted from an intellectualized attitude of his adulthood. He grew up believing women should stay on their pedestals, and he never really threw aside this feeling. Most women in his stories were thoroughly humanized, if not humbled or degraded. They were weak or deluded. Even so, and always, Cooper affirmed their human dignity.

When Madison Cooper molded into the story a residence derisively called the Elliott Hotel, he modeled it after his own home—changing the tan brick to gray frame. The interior of the Sironia house, however, was different from 1801 Austin Avenue and the inhabitants were nothing like his parents, or himself.

When he established the interesting ancestry of Sironia's leading characters, he included a story he had heard occurred in Tennessee. This dealt with a mother who daily went to the tomb to oil and comb her dead daughter's hair.

Drawing on his knowledge of United States financial history, he used the names Storrow, Reardon, and Hayden from Boston. Later he changed Hayden to Haydn.

To cement the reality of his story into the reader's mind, he kept within easy reach a catalog of events during the years covered in his novel—from the U.S. depression of 1898 through the Titanic disaster of 1912, to Prohibition in 1920 when the Eighteenth Amendment went into effect.

Caleb Hone, Cooper's newspaper editor in Sironia, was given the
role of a canny and brilliant Yankee with incisive perspective. Hone
could see straight through small-town Sironian vice and pretensions.
Interestingly, as Hone's insight deepened, he loved Sironia and its
people more. His comment on the action serves as a kind of Greek
chorus to the tidal wave of life. One of his most telling conclusions
is one of several themes of the long novel. It came when he observed that the easily seeded, fast-growing hackberry tree symbolized
the rising society of "average" people who were taking over the once
quality-dominated city. Hone likened the old aristocracy of the
South to the magnolia. Once cut down, it is a long, long time being
replaced, for it grows slowly. From the Sironia editor's window
overlooking the square, Hone saw the magnolia and hackberry—
very much as Cooper of Waco could see the same trees from his
third-floor office. A hackberry in his own yard shaded his office
window from the morning sun; across the street he could glimpse
a tall magnolia casting its shadow on the Waco Public Library.

When he wrote of automobiles in Sironia, he supported his memory with information gleaned in 1947 from the *Investor's Reader*.
This magazine renewed his personal acquaintance with such extinct
automobiles as the Ace, the Pierce-Arrow, and the Jordan.

Cooper researched facts about World War I. He ordered his
Civil War battles into place so his Sironian children could play war
games. He solidified his view of the past with such articles as "The
Changing Face of Main Street," written by a midwesterner in *Advertising and Selling* in 1946.

A telephone repairman going into his office once in the mid-1940s
found himself wading ankle-deep in wadded paper on the floor, the
result of the rewriting which sometimes took place as many as twenty
times on the tough passages. Cooper cut over 200,000 words from
the novel before completion.[9]

Many of his friends in Waco were getting the standard brush-off.
He rarely went to parties, although by his own admission parties had
once been a consuming interest. Keeping to himself, he rushed from
one fixed chore to another on his unvarying schedule, jogged the
three miles weekly, and explained himself to no one. His head was
too full of the lives he controlled on paper. By 1947 the novel
bristled with twenty-one interwoven plots and subplots. These he
described as plot threads on a page labeled Suspense List. Conflicts or unanswered questions introduced early in the story were

not unraveled for the reader until hundreds of thousands of words later.

The unprinted back of six legal size stock comment sheets from his brokers provided him with space for an outline of *The Hills of Sironia.* On these he worked out the detailed chronology of events and indicated the work consisted of *fifty-three* chapters. Thus Merrill Lynch, Pierce, Fenner & Beane served him again, in a way they would never imagine.

The photographs on these two pages are of Madison Alexander Cooper, Jr., through childhood. The last in the series was made when he was a student at the University of Texas. Observe the similarity of his expression at all ages.

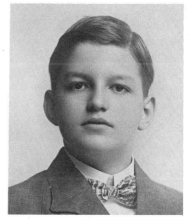
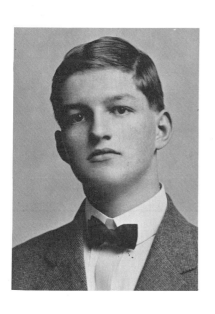

Madison Cooper dressed in his old clothes. This was not the local popula-tion's idea of how a rich man should appear in public, but he did not care.

His publisher requested candid photographs showing buildings and countryside similar to what Madison Cooper saw when he imagined Sironia, Texas. The author sent this 1952 photograph of a house in Waco at Second and Jefferson Avenue, and wrote these words: "This shows the sad state of one-time glory. Prior to their abolishment in 1917, this was for many years Waco's foremost whorehouse. The Choo Choo House [in Sironia] was of the same 'architecture' but not exactly like this. Little is left of this structure but the outside walls."

In 1952 Madison Cooper told his publisher, "South Fork Cemetery [in Sironia] could have looked like the above. Note individual lot fencing of brick, wire, and wrought iron pickets. This is Waco's oldest cemetery, the scene of a 1951 grave-desecration by a group of happy 'teenagers' expressing themselves." This cemetery was restored in 1968 by the City of Waco and in 1971 is called Fort Fisher Historic Cemetery.

Here is Madison Cooper on the red cinder track at Waco Municipal Stadium where he usually worked out three times weekly, and where he ran his last mile in 1956.

An impressive family monument selected by Madison Cooper's mother dominates the large lot in Oakwood Cemetery in Waco where the author was buried in 1956. Small headstones mark the graves of Mr. and Mrs. Cooper, Madison, and Christine who died in childhood.

The sturdy, ornate mansion built by his father early in the twentieth century which was Matt Cooper's home all of his adult life. The gabled roof at the right is over his attic office where he wrote his novels. He read books and galley proofs in the cupola, but did not write there.

Madison Cooper called this photograph made for Sironia, Texas *promotion* "The Streetwalkers Hamlet." *Date: 1952. Age: 58 years.*

Madison Cooper in his cluttered office in 1952. Sironia genealogy chart and town map is on the wall in front of him. He kept files in metal filing cabinets, bureau drawers, and cardboard boxes.

IX *Troubled Family Business*

EXCEPT FOR MODEST sums realized from fiction sales in 1926, 1936, and 1939, Madison Cooper's investment income had constituted his entire earnings since the days when he ceased drawing a salary from the Cooper Grocery Company, Inc. Investments led him into urgent consideration of the company's methods of operation in 1947. Trouble lay ahead.

Madison Cooper, Jr., had held his connection with his father's wholesale merchandising company lightly from the time he was elected secretary of the board of directors February 14, 1920. His corporate duties were few; his personal interest in management of the enterprise was nil. After his father's death in 1940, he wrote a memorandum to President J. R. Milam and Vice-President and General Manager U. C. Sterquell:

> I never expect to go back [to active participation in the company], except in close interest as a stockholder and for family reasons.[1]

Seven years later those considerations pulled him into the growing problems of a dying concern. He became a major participant in a tormented sequence of maneuvering and litigation that resulted in the end of the Cooper Company, Incorporated.

It was the accidental death of U. C. Sterquell which compelled Madison Cooper to reconsider his company obligations. Sterquell's absence at company offices turned loose a whir of dissension. For years Sterquell had kept upper-level disagreement from entangling company operations. He stilled the waters not so much with any peacemaking diplomacy as with his own sure grasp of the wholesale grocery business. An articulate and intelligent man, Sterquell with his knowledge and rationalism untied the crippling knots of discord, but a highway accident ended the prudent moratorium he engineered between two management factions headed by Edward Clay Barrett and Jesse Rush Milam, Sr.

Madison Cooper was then pulled into the breach to protect certain investments. The first was his own five hundred and seventy shares of company stock. More important than his money, however, was his investment in sentiment attached to the company in which he was reared, and which bore his family name. He never used the word *sentiment* in this connection; instead he said "for family reasons." Another investment of great importance was his lifelong friendship with Ed Barrett, who was eighty-one in 1947. He was Madison Cooper's senior by twenty-eight years, but Madison would always side with Ed Barrett.

An Old Hushed Rift

When the first Madison Cooper started wholesaling apples and potatoes out of a railroad car with the help of a Negro, Morris Wood, in 1879, he chose one of the most promising growth opportunities in a growing economy. As the country settled up with farmers and farm village merchants, the demand for the services of a wholesale food purveyor multiplied. M. A. Cooper thrived, first as an individual merchant, then by 1884 as M. A. Cooper and Co., which in 1892 bought out Moore Bros. wholesale grocers and moved into the Moore Bros. building at Fourth Street and Mary Avenue in South Waco. In 1897, M. A. Cooper, E. C. Barrett, and H. K. Brewer incorporated the Cooper Grocery Company to solidify and further exploit the business of feeding a large portion of the population of Central Texas.

In less than three years the Cooper Grocery Company established branch houses at Hillsboro and Temple, thirty-five miles north and south of Waco respectively, and within a few more years added branch houses at Taylor, Cleburne, and Gatesville. The merchandise rolled to customer stores by rail and by mule-drawn wagons. A coffee roasting plant at Waco added to the profitable inventory and Cooper's Best Coffee dominated the local market.

In 1907, two experienced wholesale grocerymen, Jesse R. Milam and Henry W. Carver, bought interests in the Cooper Grocery Company, and became, respectively, vice-president and treasurer. After World War I, while Madison A. Cooper, Jr., was trying to act like a grocery company executive for his father, U. C. Sterquell joined the organization. Youngest of the management group, he rose to the rank of vice-president and general manager. E. C. Barrett continued as vice-president with a primary responsibility for the buying and selling of goods.

The goods kept moving and the money flowed in; the eye-shaded bookkeepers perched on high stools kept pushing their steel pens across the Boston ledgers. The cavernous warehouses, redolent of coffee, spices, and foodstuffs, answered the housewives' demands as reflected in orders from the hundreds of retail grocers who depended on the Cooper Grocery Company, Incorporated for supplies. The Cooper building at Fourth and Mary was expanded, remodeled, and dressed up with red brick and white stone facing. The company bought more space at Fifth and Jackson. Stock was split, and split again, and dividends always were paid on the dot. Snorting trucks replaced the huge drays and their sleek mules, but that was almost the only concession to the technological progress of the 1920s and 1930s in the Cooper empire.

Boll weevil, drought, and depressed farm prices in the 1920s afflicted King Cotton's Central Texas empire, but people still were able to eat and Cooper warehouses continued to flourish. As the Great Depression came on and the first experimental chain stores invaded the grocery business, hardly a ripple of change washed over the Cooper operation. In 1931, the company added a line of dry goods and changed the firm's name in 1934 to the Cooper Company, Incorporated, when the new addition proved profitable. But the same old patterns of business, financing, and personnel management continued in the snug Cooper buildings in Waco, Temple, Hillsboro, Taylor, Cleburne, and Gatesville.

Edward C. Barrett, the original vice-president, typified the Cooper style. Formal, precise, orderly, dedicated, and businesslike, this North Carolina bachelor tried to keep all those qualities in the people on the payroll. He barely tolerated smoking. He fired any employee known to use alcohol to excess. Nobody within range of his ear ever used another employee's first name. It was "Mr." or "Miss" or "Mrs." Besides setting the tone for the Cooper offices, Mr. Ed, as his fellow-townsmen called him, had a fatherly affection for Madison Cooper, Jr., and a deep respect for the younger Cooper's intelligence and integrity.

There never was close rapport between Vice-President Barrett (1897) and Vice-President Milam (1907). Mr. Milam never forgot the panic of 1920–21 when Mr. Barrett's inventory, bought before the price break that followed World War I, went for postpanic prices. The loss, estimated at $200,000, was a shock to which the Cooper empire was not accustomed. The fact that the shock was temporary did not soften Mr. Milam's memory of it.

When M. A. Cooper gave up the presidency of his firm in 1938 to accept a newly minted title, chairman of the board of directors, Henry W. Carver had become the principal individual stockholder and was elected president. He never had time to relish the title, for sudden illness cut him down April 30 following his election in February. J. R. Milam succeeded to the presidency on May 17, 1938.

Through the war years and the Central Texas prosperity that went with them, U. C. Sterquell emerged as the strong man of the Cooper organization. As vice-president and general manager he kept the peace and moved the goods but even he could not change the ponderous way of operating a business still geared to the age of steam and the mule-drawn wagon. Whether he could have streamlined Cooper methods to compete with the new supermarket operations that by-passed the jobber is a matter for speculation. Coming home from a vacation trip with his son, U. C. Sterquell was killed in an automobile accident in Oklahoma September 17, 1947. This left the aging Milam, seventy-eight, and Barrett, eighty-one, an unwilling team who could not work together with any real agreement, to face a revolutionary time in the wholesale merchandise field. The small retailers who had been the backbone of the Cooper wholesale business since 1879 had been going under in large numbers for a decade. The Cooper firm had been famous for extending credit to them at 8 percent, and equally famous for collection techniques used by M. A. Cooper himself, and later by J. R. Milam, who personally hounded the unfortunate merchants for money before the last resort of foreclosure.

In addition, when numerous retail grocers could not retire their debts, the Waco wholesaler added to its business procedure by purchasing notes and accounts into the hundreds of thousands of dollars. The company acquired such notes and past-due accounts with the intention of using its strength to collect, or renew and continually secure the debts[2] until they got paid. This activity put the Cooper Grocery Company in the loan business.

With the death of U. C. Sterquell, Vice-President Barrett turned to Madison A. Cooper, Jr., seeking leadership for the floundering company. Cooper was elevated from secretary to first vice-president in 1948 and found himself in the center of the storm. His successor as secretary was Jesse R. Milam, Jr., son of the elderly president, a young man marked by Barrett and Cooper as having much promise as a leader in the future.

Madison Cooper edged back into the business and summed it up

in a resumé of problems there: "The situation is full of unlit dyna-
mite."

This era in his career best illustrates a Cooper characteristic—
his devotion to principle as opposed to expediency. In 1948 he was
concerned with the rules corporate management should follow. At
first he tried to work with the company's board of directors. He
wanted to convince them that net quick assets (cash and its equivalent
plus receivables, or current assets less inventory) should exceed
current liabilities. The directors apparently were unmoved by his
financial views. President Milam in a meeting told Cooper he was
wrong, and the subject was closed. In the same directors' meeting
Cooper suggested the company could improve its position with the
banks and the stockholders by reducing its inventory and putting
the cash into U.S. treasury bonds. He reported to Barrett that the
secretary of the board laughed at this, and said, "I know we don't
want to do that."[3] The rebuff confounded Cooper. He would not
press to the point of open argument which might be picked up by
the public, convinced as he was that any kind of talk was bad for
business.

Two concurrent plans to solve company problems were devised
privately and put in black on white by the careful planner, Madison
Cooper. As always, he started from an idea and worked it out fully
to the last alternative. First he would attempt to set up what he
called an accident-proof management organization within the present
corporate ownership. By accident proof, he meant that death of a
key man would not hinder company work. As he advanced toward
these plans, he dropped hints to possible buyers of the Cooper
Company.

To prepare for sale of the company, Madison Cooper typed a
memorandum for himself to follow in negotiating a possible sale:

Any deal of any kind to which I may be a party will be arrived at
openly, so far as other stockholders are concerned, *all* of them having
any sale opportunity I may have. . . . Should I work out this or any
other deal, I neither expect nor want any commission. This is not
my business . . .

My belief: one of several courses should be chosen while we are
not under pressure, while Company is doing *fine* [the company's credit
rating was still good] rather than wait until sudden death, or accident
puts us in a crucial position.

Jesse, Jr., has made a good start, is serious about his work, happily married. He is about thirty and has had only about four years actual experience in the business. It is quite possible that in another ten years —by the time his father has to give up active work—he will be capable of taking over—if we knew Mr. Milam would last that long.

Shortly, a flutter of circumspect letters passed between Cooper and Kay Kimbell of Fort Worth, then owner of about thirty corporations, chiefly, but not entirely, in the foods industry from manufacturing to distribution. Kimbell would become a player in the Cooper Co. drama. He met with Cooper at 1801 Austin Avenue and later offered to buy the grocery merchandise at cost or market, whichever was lower, expecting a 2 percent discount. Kimbell would also buy buildings, trucks—and accounts, "with your firm's guarantee." Or, Kimbell wrote, he might buy the corporation's stock at an advantageous price.[4]

Kay Kimbell might that fall of 1948 have had one less wholesale competitor, except that he delayed, and by the time he made his counter offer Madison A. Cooper, Jr., had decided to provide his personal financial backing to the troubled company. Provided he and Barrett could gain control. This they did when on January 24, 1949, Mrs. H. W. Carver, widow of the company's second president, signed a proxy agreement to last five years. Thus, the Barrett interests gained control of the company, with Madison calling the turn.

Madison's Methods

To open up company control from that of a single executive to several stockholders, Madison Cooper weakened the presidency and strengthened an executive committee consisting of four stockholders. Internal strife was no secret as Barrett became chairman of the committee. The other members were J. R. Milam who retained his title, but whose power was leveled to one vote, the same as the remaining two members, Madison Cooper and Henry Carter. To invoke the help he knew the committee needed, Cooper had with him on that changeover day a prayer by Chaplain Peter Marshall of the U.S. Senate:

O God, our Father, let us not be content to wait and see what will happen, but give us the determination to make the Right things happen.

A month-long discussion about bringing new blood into the company ended in action when Cooper sent advertising copy to the *Wall Street Journal* Southwest edition in Dallas: "Needed now: A general manager by a large Texas wholesaler of groceries: Preferably about 40 years of age, with an excellent record as to character, ability, experience in this field and for results."[5] The advertisement brought results. Seventeen men applied for the job, chiefly as a result of this and a *Dallas Morning News* insertion, but after receiving a letter from R. B. Hoover of McKinney, Texas, most of the other applicants looked unpromising to Madison Cooper. He followed up on only one other inquiry.

Madison Cooper did not act on a hunch. He had Robert Bradley Hoover thoroughly investigated. The recommendations indicated that Hoover in character, ability, and work habits was virtually peerless. From Cooper's hard sell of his first choice of general manager trainee (he would start as a troubleshooter) it was difficult to tell whether he was most pleased that Hoover was unreservedly recommended by both McKinney banks, or whether he liked best the fact that Hoover was a second-generation wholesale grocer. All considered, R. B. Hoover, fourteen years his junior, was the kind of man Cooper could watch develop into the executive material he needed. The executive committee hired Hoover with plans to work him into the general manager's title in about five years, sooner if possible.

Efficiency and Austerity

The executive committee made changes to cut overhead and extract maximum production from existing assets and employees. In so doing the committee carried out founder M. A. Cooper's edict: "Your competitors control your percentage of gross profit, but you in managing your expense account can control your net profits."[7]

During this time Madison Cooper got wind of slander directed at the Cooper Foundation. Such talk infuriated him, but he knew there is no effective way to beat out such public grassfires and he knew such talk is often started by influential enemies. He reasoned that by signing an affidavit he would preserve in print what he held to be the truth:

COOPER FOUNDATION was created by me in good faith as a memorial to my beloved and esteemed parents. It was never—in any sense—"a tax-dodging pretext," as an ignorant and possibly malicious few may—or may not—have stated. COOPER FOUNDATION should be above even unwarranted suspicion to accomplish the most good.

After nearly a year of silence, a friendly business letter came to Waco from Kay Kimbell of Fort Worth. "Haven't heard from you in a long time." he began.[8]

Madison Cooper replied that the company had put in a new plan of management. The results, he said, were gratifying. *Hopeful* would have been a better word. The Cooper Company, Inc., operated at a slight loss in 1949 and the early months of 1950. Early in 1950 Cooper voluntarily stopped drawing the small salary he earned as vice-chairman of the executive committee. And several months later, Barrett reduced his own salary by over two-thirds. This reversed a long-standing policy. In years gone by salary cuts were borne by subordinates.

Money Sources Retreat

Four sources of operating capital had funded the company business operations—(1) earned surplus (working capital), (2) loans from stockholders' deposit accounts, (3) loans obtained from big banks, and (4) loans obtained from sale of commercial paper (company notes) peddled by brokers who make their living in this way. The Cooper Company's foreign banking connections had long been the Boatmen's National Bank of Saint Louis and the Chase National Bank of New York City. Its commercial paper broker was F. S. Moseley and Co., a Boston-based firm which did business with Waco through its Chicago house.

If they wanted to, these banks and brokers could bring the company to its knees in humility. In 1950 they united to do so, chiefly at the implied suggestion of the National Credit Office located on New York City's Park Avenue. This investors' watchdog had been waiting to see what the strife-ridden Waco concern would do next. When the National Credit Office obtained the company audit mailed out in early 1950, the New Yorkers blacklisted the Cooper Company, Inc. Banks, other investors, commercial paper brokers had the word: ACCOUNT IS NOT RECOMMENDED AS AN OPEN MARKET INVESTMENT. This was black news indeed.

After analyzing the company's position as of January 31, 1950, the National Credit office with five damning facts asserted that "borrowings [by the Cooper Company] should be confined to those in a position to follow the affairs of the company closely." The New York office justified its damnation when it pointed out that (1) the company's working capital dropped by $78,000 [operating loss was only $7,891; the board had voted $70,000 in dividends for stockholders], (2) the company's indebtedness increased to 83 percent of its net worth, (3) inventories increased by $85,000 in the face of a 10 percent sales drop, (4) regular dividends were paid in spite of an operating loss, and (5) reduction of $64,000 in deposits due officers and stockholders (implying a loss of confidence on the part of such officials and investors).

As a direct result of this, F. S. Moseley and Co. returned a $100,-000 block of Cooper Co. notes payable to the Chase National Bank of New York.

Prior to this turn of events, Madison Cooper foresaw that management change and decreasing profits might hurt the company's standing, so he had already investigated other ways to finance the operation.[9] Yet he couldn't be certain when it would happen, and the situation grew urgent because the company had debts to pay which would require borrowed money. The Cooper Company, Inc., was humiliated further as one after another lending institution declined to put up the money needed.

A letter from Waco to the National Credit Office reflected a defensive posture loathed by all the executives. The spot where National Credit had hurt Madison Cooper most was the fiscal year-end dividend (10 percent on each share at $100 par value) paid out of the earned surplus when the company failed to show a profit. Cooper now realized this was a serious error. And the responsibility for it must be shared by himself and the committee. Some of the executive committee members had urged paying the unearned dividends because the money was needed. The president, J. R. Milam, had urged that it be paid because he was proud of the company's record of never missing a dividend.

Madison Cooper cared less about both justifications than he did his new profit sharing plan for all employees. Called incentive bonus, this pet project would pay off to employees only if the company declared stockholders' dividends. Madison Cooper believed he was doing right by the employees who depended on him. For these reasons the executive committee rationalized that the earned surplus built up in good years could stand the strain. The members knew that dividends twice had been paid partly out of the earned surplus in previous years.

Madison Cooper was forced to share the responsibility for the reduction in deposit accounts, another weakness cited by the National Credit Office. He had withdrawn $50,000 to invest at higher interest than the 2 percent paid on open account by the Cooper Company. Even at that, he with $79,000 remaining in the deposit account, Barrett with $64,592, and Mrs. H. W. Carver with $100,086 were the three big depositors in 1950.

Madison Cooper was the only one in the company with financial strength needed to save the Cooper Company, Inc., from bankruptcy. Convinced that he must relent for the good of the company, he turned to a local institution, the Citizens National Bank of Waco, which arranged loans with the First National Bank of Waco and First National of Dallas. Madison Cooper's name went on the line guaranteeing many hundreds of thousands of dollars. Barrett and Milam joined him in the endorsements, but Cooper stood to lose the most.

During this troubled time the executive committee tried to regard casually Mrs. H. W. Carver's telephone call saying her relatives were urging her to get her money out of the company. Cooper told her that she could draw out her big deposit any time she presented the note she held against the company—but didn't she always defer such a step, saying she did not want to make a decision just yet? This was a crucial subplot boiling beneath the surface of company problems.

Then another letter came from Fort Worth to Madison Cooper. Kay Kimbell began, "Haven't heard from you in some time. The grocery business is getting a little tougher for us all the time."[10] Madison responded:

> Your summary of the grocery business is a good one. There just isn't enough profitable business for all of the jobbers now operating in each territory. . . . As you say, some of them will be eliminated, but I don't think the Cooper Company will be among them.
> The only meeting you and I ever had—almost two years ago—keeps cropping up as having occurred *recently*. Just a few weeks back we were reported to have held a conference in the Raleigh Hotel here.[11]

Happily, after the bleak period of losses in early 1950, profits soared late in the year to give the executive committee renewed confidence, but not intemperance. R. B. Hoover was moved up to assistant general manager and the fiscal year-end stockholder bulletin announced the company was operating in the black:

> Your company had a good year in 1950, a *very* good year, everything considered. The book value of your stock is now approximately $9.00 per share more than it was a year ago. Gratifying, indeed, are the numerous compliments the Company has received recently on our greatly improved financial position. . . . The present management is in full agreement with its financial advisors that all this year's profits be plowed back into building working capital to where it should be. . . . For this reason, the board of directors has voted to omit the dividend for this year. . . . Your company is in good financial condition.[12]

Among moves Madison Cooper made in 1950 to gain a firm hold on the Cooper Company, Inc. was retaining a Waco law firm he trusted implicitly, Naman, Howell, and Boswell. The firm replaced Witt, Terrell, Jones, and Riley, long-time company attorneys preferred by the Milam family.

A special meeting of the board of directors was called to express the company's sympathy for the bereaved family of J. R. Milam, president for twelve years, vice-president from 1907, who died at the age of eighty-one years.

The board's resolution:

> The [board of directors'] motion carried the firm's appreciation of the deceased's forty-three years of service with it and its highest commendation of his many personal benefactions, only a few of which are generally known.[13]

This would be another turning point in Cooper Co. events.

X *End of The Cooper Co., Inc.*

NOT EVERYONE SHARED the executive committee's good feeling in 1951 about the improved status of quick assets over current liabilities, although it was a fine boost to Madison Cooper's confidence. When the board of directors, consisting chiefly of Barrett interests leaning on the judgment of Cooper, voted to turn all earnings back into working capital, the loss of dividends was bad news in other quarters. Coupled as it was with J. R. Milam's death, a resulting loss of salary, his son J. R. Milam, Jr., was forced to look about more earnestly in behalf of himself and his mother. The Milam family obligation to protect its long-standing interest and equity in the company was solely his.

J. R. Milam, Jr., known to Madison Cooper as Jesse, told Cooper that if the executive committee failed to pay the next year's dividends also that Mrs. Milam, widow of the late president, would run short of funds. Cooper held out unsympathetically during the conference, but two days later he relented and informed Milam that the company might buy back enough of Mrs. Milam's stock at par value to tide her over. During a twelve-month period after such a purchase, Cooper said, Mrs. Milam could regain the same stock at the same price plus 6 percent interest. Milam, taking a dim view of this suggestion, looked around for a better and more satisfactory answer.

Cooper had never spent but an hour or two daily at the company offices where now dissatisfaction pushed up a new ground swell of dissension. Barrett, probably more intolerant of human weakness and the changing times than ever, was president. The employees fretted under restraints of reduced overhead and the futility of selling millions of dollars worth of groceries while getting no return themselves for their increased interest or painful adjustments to change. Even the first promising incentive bonus had been spent and forgotten. The executive committee had given itself five years to restore the company. Only two had passed.

To add to the executive committee's burden, Mrs. H. W. Carver was now writing letters to Cooper and Barrett demanding that they release her from the five-year proxy agreement on which depended their voting control of the company. She also called Cooper on the telephone to tell him that W. E. Terrell, a member of their displaced law firm, had asked if she would sell her Cooper stock. She responded negatively at first. Almost immediately she changed her mind. At the time Madison did not connect Mrs. Carver's dissatisfaction with Jesse Milam, Jr.

Needless to say, Cooper held her to the proxy agreement, which soon initiated a letter from a Dallas attorney (Mrs. Carver's brother-in-law) saying Mrs. Carver considered she had the right to cancel her proxy, and she was so doing. Hilton E. Howell, Cooper's attorney, then notified the lawyer that the proxy was irrevocable. When the Dallas lawyer threatened suit[1] Cooper requested a meeting with Kay Kimbell in Fort Worth. Kimbell's response was so casual that Cooper began to see the outline of a puzzle and called off the trip, but his information was too sketchy to piece out the picture.

Because Madison Cooper had a lifelong, overriding distaste for public attention, he released Mrs. Carver's proxy. He was convinced that a suit reported in the newspapers and publicly discussed, however unfounded the accusations might be, would seriously damage the Cooper Company. And he believed a court trial would further weaken Ed Barrett. The Cooper Company, Inc., paid off all obligations to Mrs. Carver. Only then did Madison Cooper learn that "an unnamed party" had obtained an option to buy Mrs. Carver's shares at par, provided the proxy was released. Now, Madison Cooper began to understand the logic of Mrs. Carver's actions.

Then on August 24, 1951, Madison Cooper got the kind of surprise that the Milam family had experienced earlier. Jesse R. Milam, Jr., informed Cooper that he owned the Carver shares and now controlled the company. He left the door open for resignations from the executive committee, including the new assistant general manager Hoover who would never get the job he came to Waco for; Naman, Howell, and Boswell lost a legal account; and Milam would put the old president-manager system back into operation ending E. C. Barrett's brief tenure as company head.

As fast as possible, Cooper canceled his surety for company loans, salvaged such company privileges as he could, and put in a long distance telephone call to Kay Kimbell. Would he buy? Kimbell said he would like to buy the grocery inventory just as he had offered in 1948, but he didn't want the dry goods. As Madison Cooper remembered it later, Kimbell claimed he knew nothing of Jesse Milam's new controlling interest.[2] The call to Kimbell resulted in a note Cooper wrote to Jesse Milam advising sale of the grocery inventory—to solve many company problems. Taking the defeat in good faith, Cooper and Barrett kept their stock, retained their company loyalty, and held hopes that the company would prosper. In a called meeting of Cooper-Barrett supporters, all agreed that if asked, they would say that Milam had control and since his policies did not agree with those of Cooper and Barrett, that those two had "quite amicably" retired from management of the business.[3]

This period of August, 1951, to February, 1952—one half of one year—covers more unpalatable surprises than Madison Cooper could digest. Not only did J. R. Milam, Jr., a man half his age, now control the company Madison Cooper tried to save, not only did this Milam go against Cooper's considered advice, but Kay Kimbell was revealed to be the money source behind Milam's power play.

What Happened?

Madison Cooper and his colleagues began to put the pieces together. The only significant observation made during the past months had been notice of pronounced recalcitrance in young Milam. In July, 1951, unknown to the controlling executive committee, Milam had gone to Fort Worth to confer with Kay Kimbell. About the same time, with W. E. Terrell's help, Milam obtained an option on Mrs. H. W. Carver's 1105 shares at par. But he also needed the nine hundred shares owned by eight Carver heirs. Their price was high—two for one, or $200 per share. With his own family's 1511 shares, he would have control, provided he could get the necessary financing.

Kimbell agreed to provide him the funds, about $290,600 at 4 percent. But he had his conditions: (1) Milam must sell out the entire grocery, coffee, and spice departments, ending forever the old company's first purpose, (2) Milam must sign a six-month *demand* note for the entire sum, (3) the newly purchased shares must be collateral, (4) Kimbell buyers would have first refusal of the grocery inventory. Milam planned to pay off part of his note to Kimbell with capital he believed would result from sale of the grocery inventory and equipment. This he expected to bring in a million dollars or more to be distributed among the stockholders.

Count your chickens before they hatch! Not only did the liquidation fail to bring as much as the young president expected, but also the company auditors, the Dallas office of Ernst and Ernst, informed him that the company then could not make such a capital distribution without approval by two-thirds majority of all stockholders. Milam rightly believed the chances of getting either Cooper's or Barrett's approval on this were worse than nil.

For a while it appeared that Kimbell had a big block of Cooper shares (Milam's collateral), for when Milam pressed Kimbell to pay for groceries that the Kimbell Grocery Company had bought, he balked. Too much money moving around, he said. So he moved with the freedom a demand note allows and called it in two months early. At the time Kimbell owed the Cooper Company about $300,-000 for liquidation purchases.

When Kimbell chose not to wait the full six months, he put his debtor in the bind of a lifetime. Now what? Where would the money come from to pay Kimbell?

Cooper Seeks Information

Madison Cooper had no direct pipeline from company affairs that fateful fall, but he intended to find out what was going on. He still felt he had obligations to the other minority stockholders, as well as himself. In addition, from the moment he heard of Kimbell's involvement, Cooper was edgy and suspicious.

To get the help he had long needed to manage his various affairs, Madison Cooper employed R. B. Hoover whom he had personally influenced to come to Waco. Hoover's new job would be to manage Cooper's commercial real estate and assist him with the increasing role of the growing Cooper Foundation. The foundation's assets were now well past the quarter million mark.

In addition Madison Cooper wanted to keep up with the fiscal state of Cooper Company affairs, and who would be better qualified to interpret company books than the firm's former assistant general manager?[4] The company books disclosed that the new president had signed a note to borrow nearly a third of a million dollars from the Cooper Company, Inc., income account, a fund which in Madison's mind had become a sacred vessel for restoring the good name of the company. The money went to Kay Kimbell to pay off Jesse R. Milam, Jr.'s debt.

Cooper's rage and indignation climbed out of sight. He double-checked his personal cash reserve to determine how far he might go in the courts to right what he believed was a fathomless wrong. Throwing his old concern for public opinion to the winds, he determined to sue; he had the funds, and he would fight to the last ditch; he wanted to strip the present management of every vestige of ownership and control. To Howell and Hoover he outlined a civil action to be brought by the minority stockholders. It would be initiated against their opponent not for themselves alone, but in behalf of the company.[5] Its aim would be recovery of the loan, or the 2005 shares put up as collateral. What's more he hoped for a judgment to recover what he claimed was excessive compensation for the president's services, including a commission Milam was receiving for arranging the sale of the grocery inventory.[6] Simultaneously the new board of directors ended Madison Cooper's incentive bonus plan and at the same meeting voted to give no dividends for fiscal 1951, ironically carrying out the act it feared Cooper would perform—had he remained in control.[7]

Court Contention Makes News[8]

COOPER FIRM
CONTROL SUIT
TO OPEN HERE

A $320,000 suit set in Judge D. Y. McDaniel's 74th District Court Monday may change again the course of history of the Cooper Company, Inc., rocked in recent years by convulsive changes.

A petition filed last February [now mid-May] attacks company control and asks the court to set aside a $292,954.33 loan, a commission exceeding $22,000, and the president's salary. Plaintiffs in the suit hold 3000 shares; defendants hold 3032. The remaining 968 of 7000 shares of capital stock are now treasury stock recently bought in by the company at $146 from three stockholders preferring to avoid the contention, and from J. R. Milam, Jr.

Among answers from the defendants will be Milam's statements that he did not borrow from the company any money he used to purchase his 2005 shares of stock. The defendants will further claim it is not outside the corporation charter to make such loans. They will contend the stock purchase was purely private and proper and they will try to show that the president's duties do not cover sale of the grocery division.

KIMBELL LOAN
IN COOPER CO.
DEAL IS AIRED

. . . the court heard Milam say today that he told Kimbell he would pay off part of the debt with a capital distribution resulting from the grocery, coffee, and spice sellout. He said no agreement was made as to how the money would be repaid; or how he could get the debt refinanced.

HOWELL, NAMAN
TO REST CASE
IN COURT TODAY

JURY SUPPORTS
BARRETT, ET AL
IN COOPER TIFF

The jury phase of the trial ended today when the twelve men reached a decision on the one issue submitted to them. They ruled the market value of Cooper Company stock is $100 a share supporting the argument of the plaintiffs. Defendants argued it is worth considerably more.

Judge McDaniel held that the legality of the loan is a question of law. He asked the plaintiffs' attorneys, W. W. Naman and Hilton E. Howell, and the defense firm of Witt, Terrell, Jones and Riley, to submit briefs on which he will hear arguments before he renders a judgment.

COURT UPHOLDS
COOPER STAND

Judge D. Y. McDaniel of the 74th District Court ruled Wednesday that the Cooper Company, Inc., had no right to loan $292,594.33 to its president, Jesse R. Milam, Jr. The judge said Milam would have to pay back the money to the company, or lose the stock with which he secured the loan—which would mean loss of control of the company.

The suit was brought by minority stockholders, listing first E. C. Barrett whose death occurred May 30, a week and two days after the trial ended.

The judge ruled against the plaintiffs on two points. He will not require the defendant to restore either the commission for disposing of the grocery inventory or his salary.

Hilton E. Howell, lawyer for the plaintiffs now designated as Cooper, et al, said after the present suit is settled another will be prepared to regain attorneys' fees from the losers.

To outside observers it would seem a total victory for Cooper, et al. A moral victory it was. A basic victory in behalf of the company's integrity, it was. A decisive victory for the executive committee, it was not. First, the court declined to award punitive damages as the plaintiffs asked. Second, Milam still controlled the corporation, and he kept the new, higher salary, and the $22,000 commission for selling all grocery stock.

Neither he nor his advisors were asleep at the switch. Milam had a choice before him which could make him the ultimate winner—if indeed such a distinction were possible. Milam would stay ahead if he could retain his early gains. This could be accomplished if he could repay the money he had borrowed from the company.

Why not liquidate part of the capital stock? This tactic would be a pro-rata cash payment to every stockholder, winner and loser alike, out of the capital stock account. Such a move would mean paying out to stockholders a portion of the $700,000 mother lode stored in the company under the aegis of Madison Cooper's father as president. It had been stored, and used over and over again to conduct company business since 1922—thirty years ago. This proposed partial capital liquidation in 1952 would chip away at the core of the corporation—mining money put there during the company's heyday. Yet, why get sentimental about the capital stock? Madison Cooper, Jr., was fully capable of grasping the advisability of a partial liquidation, but he was particular about who made the decision. Further, he knew this partial company liquidation would keep company reins in Milam's hands, for with his share of the liquidation, he could pay part of his debt to the company.

Such a capital reduction could be effected only with the approval of ownership of two-thirds of the stock. If the Barrett heirs would join Milam interests in approving a liquidation of part of the capital stock, Milam would be on his way out of the woods. Actually, this should have been a moot question after examining Ed Barrett's will. Mr. Ed had anticipated his share votes would be decisive in the contention after his death, so he willed their *voting privileges* to Madison Cooper, Jr. Again Mr. Ed and Madison blocked Milam's play. Cooper was very much opposed to Milam's continued control of the disputed wholesale business and was apparently in the driver's seat concerning the capital liquidation.

To counter, however, the opposition proposed that as trustee Cooper could not have the Barrett stock certificates until the Barrett estate executor cleared the estate—and the estate was still unsettled. The executor, a Waco bank, believed the best way to keep the Cooper Company, Inc., in business was to reduce its capital and let it continue to operate on a smaller scale. So, when voting time came on the partial capital liquidation, the executor planned to vote *yes*. To act legally and properly, the executor notified Cooper and his attorneys that its vote would favor partial capital liquidation.

The reaction was immediate. The minority stockholders asked for a court injunction to stop the vote. The executor backed off and attempted to return the Barrett shares to Cooper, the legal trustee. The Cooper Company executives, through whose hands the share certificates must pass en route to Madison Cooper, shot them back to the executor saying the estate was not settled, hence Cooper had not the right to their voting privileges.

The Cooper injunction failed in the district court, and the executor voted to reduce the capital stock—on the condition, it said, that it had the right to vote. The executor wisely acknowledged a controversy existed and took no high-handed stand in the matter. But the matter would not be dropped; to defeat Madison Cooper was to have a fight on your hands. As the actual liquidation vote was taken, Cooper and W. W. Naman were conferring on a second major civil suit—to nullify the executor's right to vote Ed Barrett's shares. Soon the liquidation funds were tied up by the court.

Naturally, as all of these public acts occurred, the contenders would make an attempt to settle out of court. When the Cooper contingent offered to settle the feud, such propositions consistently cleaved to four basic demands:

(1) All minority stockholders must approve any settlement.

(2) The company and/or Milam must pay off all expenses of the litigation and other costly charges of the period since the executive committee lost control.

(3) Company bank indebtedness should be paid off and the company would operate only on loans it could secure without individual financial backing.

(4) Except for irrevocable changes, everything would go back to the austere principles and methods Cooper was attempting to put into effect when the trouble began.

Just as consistently the opposition refused to reduce Milam to the salary he had drawn during Cooper's reign. And Milam refused Madison Cooper the company privileges he had enjoyed for years, including use of company office machines, parking privileges, buying at wholesale prices for personal use, and certain bookkeeping accommodations.

Both sides knew that the opposition would push any gains. Cooper wanted the company restored, but he was convinced that Milam was too inexperienced to run it. Milam wanted the company restored, but he believed that Madison Cooper would knot the organization into a hard core that would die of its own calcification.

As is often true, time was kind to both sides during the suits, appeals, and Texas Supreme Court sessions that followed.

On May 11, 1953, the Waco tornado wiped out one hundred and fourteen lives in the city and demolished business property downtown into the millions of dollars. The Cooper Company, Inc., fully insured buildings crumbled in the twister's path, but insurance payments made it possible for Milam to rebuild. Even with the business interruption insurance, the spark of life dimmed for what would one day be called the J. R. Milam Co., operating briefly as a Central and West Texas wholesale dry goods business.

Madison Cooper in three years, 1951–1954, won what he called a complete legal victory in two suits carried to the Texas Supreme Court. One was referred to as the loan case; the other they called the vote case. Of course, there were accompanying suits for attorneys' fees, which at the end favored the Cooper side entirely. But the courts never restored control of the Cooper Company to Madison. All he got was his asking price in cash for his company shares, the full cash reimbursement for all legal fees, and the assurance, given by both sides, that the court litigation was over. And perhaps most important to Madison was the final agreement that the name Cooper would be permanently struck from all buildings, trucks, and office papers. His pride in the family name caused him to insist on this final and irrevocable change. The name, Cooper, he had already attached to a growing family trust fund designed to unite the name with a happier future for the city of Waco.

Here's how the public learned it was all over in the *Waco News-Tribune* on December 9, 1954:

LONG LEGAL TANGLE OVER STOCK
IN COOPER COMPANY IS SETTLED

Change of name of Waco's fourth oldest business firm from the Cooper Company, Incorporated to the J. R. Milam Company was part of an estimated $600,000 deal ending the city's record corporate legal feud. Of this, $366,000 was a contested partial liquidation dividend voted two years ago but tied up in the courts since then.

Jesse R. Milam, Jr., 36-year-old president of the large wholesale dry goods and notions company, said the new name choice is not final. He expects the change to be made early in January, however. . . .

The long legal tug-of-war has ended with each side claiming victory. Both sides deny there is anything personal in the controversies. . . .

Cooper dictated a formal statement saying:

"All of the Cooper Company, Incorporated stock held by the minority stockholders who wanted me to act for them has been sold on a satisfactory cash basis. Mrs. Holloway Smith, Mrs. Katherine Carter Cassidy, Henry N. Carter, Jr., and Madison A. Cooper, Jr., no longer have any ownership in or connection with the company.

"By mutual agreement, the name Cooper, after a stated time, will no longer be used by the company in any way."

Cooper had told Waco newspaper reporter Chris Whitcraft that he wanted to be sure that the word "cash" got in the first sentence. "That's very important," he insisted. Whitcraft later telephoned the statement to Milam in the locker room of the local country club where he was getting ready for a round of golf.

"Succinct, isn't it?" was Milam's response.

Behind the public statements was Cooper's clear grasp of the irony of a long, bitter contest over questionable spoils. It culminated in these words from Cooper to an out-of-town friend: "By way of closing a matter several times alluded to, the long litigation by which I have been trying to get the money of the minority stockholders I represented out of the Cooper Co., Inc. has just been terminated with our side winning what a lawyer tells me is one of the clearest cut, most complete legal victories he knows of. As a result, we have been paid off in cash, the other side has to pay all of our considerable legal expense and the firm cannot use the name 'Cooper' after a stated time. Peace—with cash: it's wonderful." That last sentence, rounding off a protracted, expensive, and serious situation with a parting shot at himself, was utterly Cooperesque— the typical reaction of this man who grasped and articulated ironies, subtleties, incongruities. Being a victor, he was in good humor about the outcome. Had he lost, there can be no doubt that his raging juices of life would never have let him take it well. He entered few contests in life without expecting to win, and he took defeat poorly.

Madison had set the guidelines for goals he wanted accomplished at the end of the first of the three-year contention; he then withdrew from public view as his lawyers, Naman and Howell, carried on the suits with R. B. Hoover standing in for Madison Cooper. Although Cooper was wholly committed and followed every detail of the litigation, he also had enough free time from his business obligations to participate in his life's cherished dream which came true in 1952. It is another story which will be told next, and it runs concurrently with the end of the Cooper Company, Inc.

XI *Story of a Whole Town*

DAVID DEMPSEY OF *The New York Times* wrote a regular column entitled "In and Out of Books." Among his readers was Madison Cooper of Waco, a long-time subscriber of the Sunday *Times*. In one of his columns, written in the spring of 1951, Dempsey mentioned, almost casually, that the Houghton Mifflin Company's fellowship award application blanks awaited inquiry. Cooper, whose long novel was to be typed in triplicate by two male stenographers, decided the fellowship might be worth a try.

Feeling a little guilty about the voluminous quantity of the story he had written, the author mailed only one hundred typewritten pages with itemized information on the whole story—not a synopsis, but an explanation of seven salient points he thought the publisher needed to know. Thus Houghton Mifflin of Boston would learn that the novel's ". . . chief character is Tam Lipscomb (born in 1895), whose early life is largely conditioned by the town's (Sironia's) changeover from domination by the 'Old Order' to that of the 'New Southwest.' " While reading the three lots of typescript, they should know, Cooper thought, that "the story is one of conflict with inherited values. Although handled *lightly* here, the process is not an easy one for Tam."

Cooper wished the publisher to understand from the beginning that:

> While there is a great deal of action, some of it violent, this is primarily a novel of character. I'd like to emphasize the fact that none of the "violent" passages is used for sensational effect alone. Each is the result of what has gone before. Each marks a turning point in the story and in the life of at least one principal character. . . . I believe I have a well-sustained story of wide "popular" appeal. . . . For business reasons please keep this submission confidential.

Houghton Mifflin, believing the book unfinished, returned the three lots with the encouraging line, "However, we do like your writing and believe it shows considerable promise. We would very much appreciate a chance to see the book again when you have finished it."[1]

Then they learned that the novel was already so long that the author thought no publisher would give it a careful reading. Cooper wanted an expert editor to help him cut it down to size. Would the Boston people look at another one hundred pages or so? They would. So up to Boston went lots IV and V.

Boston publishers Houghton Mifflin Company, among the most prestigious in the business, asked for more and more manuscript of his novel. Believing the publishing firm's readers would give up with "what the hell" if sent all, Cooper self-consciously mailed three more small lots of typed material from the total of over forty batches he had already written for submission. This timidity on his part, and a reorganization in Boston which slowed the publisher's reaction, extended the important procedure of getting his literary product to the prospective buyer. At one point during 1951 Cooper thought Houghton Mifflin had lost interest and it took three widely spaced, strong nudges from the author to get a response from Boston. At last they wrote, "We are looking forward very much to seeing a more or less completed version of the manuscript."[2] They had an idea of its great length but were interested chiefly because they admired Cooper's writing. It showed the promise of a real storyteller.

As soon as he could, he shaped up his long story so that he could write with confidence:

1. Next week I am sending you by prepaid express the complete manuscript. . . . It is bound in 41 folders of (with 4 exceptions) 70 pages each. As previously stated, an overall cut of some 200,000 words is represented in this version. . . . If cut any more, I expect the result would be more a synopsis than what I seek: a novel of character with a well-sustained story implemented by action.

2. May I again emphasize two points? Although a number of its sequences are violent, they are not included for their shock value: Each results in a definite change in at least one major character. Second, while a great deal of the material (such as social distinctions, race relations, etc.) is strictly true to its time (thirty to fifty years ago), it is *not* true now and has not been for a long time. [The story spanned a score of years—1900–1921.]

He went on to affirm that he understood that the first seventy to eighty pages would bore some readers. But, he said, the pages are essential to the story. They described crucial background facts which

would influence important choices to be made by the novel's chief
character, Tam Lipscomb, as he grew up.

Cooper's heart jumped high at these words from Paul Brooks,
editor-in-chief of Houghton Mifflin, in a letter dated January 24,
1952:

> I can say at this point that we certainly shall want to publish. Everyone
> who has read the manuscript has been absorbed by it. Of course its
> length presents a formidable publishing problem . . . we shall manage
> to solve it in one way or another. . . . The ten years have not been
> wasted.

Later Cooper learned, by asking point blank, what the readers
at Houghton Mifflin thought of the novel. He knew it was on their
judgments, as well as Brooks's own, that the editor-in-chief had written "that we certainly shall want to publish."

Three readers on the Houghton Mifflin staff laid the super-novel
on the editor's desk with these reports, which Madison Cooper cherished the remaining years of his life.

One reader characterized it as the Great American Novel, while
demurring on its quality as a work of art:

> The style of this novel lies somewhere between Dreiser, Anderson,
> and the radio serial "One Man's Family," with a dash of some un-
> known original quality.

> This is a novel of time and immersion. By the time you have
> finished (it takes about a week of steady reading), you feel that you
> are a lot older and a lot more foolish.

There was a brilliant article by Edward Dahlberg in *Tomorrow
Magazine*. He said,

> The trouble with American literature is that there is no coziness—no
> wine in wicker baskets. There are just great open spaces. This novel
> remedies that.

> This is not great literature, but it is the Great American Novel. If
> I had read this outside of Houghton Mifflin, I would still have had to
> finish it. The Windex, the Simonizer, the Babo would have been left
> untouched—the woodwork would have remained dirty while I sat
> on the sofa and read and read and read.

No enthusiasm rose higher than that of the managing editor, Mrs.
Dorothy de Santillana:

> The biggest opportunity for a publishing coup since Tom Wolfe and

Ross Lockridge by a guy who knows more about life and people than either of them and whose feet seem firmly planted on the ground, indeed rooted in the earth. . . .

This novel has just about everything, but for me its unique quality is the fact that its hugeness allows it to portray things proportionately. For example, if sex is there, it isn't a novel about sex; if there are black and white relationships—and violence—it isn't a novel about the Negro problem; if there is a fine picture of self-conscious "Southern aristocracy," it isn't a novel about the Old South; if there are some marvelously done female characters, it isn't a novel about women.

This is the whole story of a town 1900–1921, its outside, its inside, its surface, its ooze below, its company manners, its off-guard moments, its people and their relations to each other. We see a generation grow up against a background which becomes more familiar than our own, we see how true the adage "child is father to the man," we see them handle inherited conditioning, adding new complexities to their own. Best of all, through the author's magnificent gift of story, we see how everything comes out—and "for the best."

For my part, I want no editing. I think every word important.

To say that Houghton Mifflin's approval of the novel pleased Cooper is an understatement. In the everyday human arena he had missed high achievement in every one of his life's conflicts and trials —until now. His late efforts to save the Cooper Company failed; his dairy farm never made much money for him; he couldn't get back into the U.S. Army during World War II on his terms; as a writer of short stories, he was undistinguished; he couldn't make the adjustment to employment at the Cooper Grocery Company; he had no wife or children; he missed his majority in the U.S. Army during the First World War and was persuaded by his parents to get out. Even in college and high school he had been only "among the best." It wasn't good enough for his own self-esteem. Madison Cooper was born with pride and perseverance so strong that no defeat this side of death could weaken them. He wrote of this characteristic in the novel when he said of the Storrows, "[they] hated weakness, right next to dishonor and discourtesy. Suppose General Hugh or Colonel Leonidas had let things that *might* happen hold them back! Blind concentration on what had to be—that was the only way."[3]

Now in 1952, at the age of fifty-eight, Madison Cooper, Jr., saw his concentration pay off in a most gratifying way in personal triumph equal to his dreams, and at an age when achievement of sudden fame is uncommon.

"The ten years [Cooper later made it clear it was closer to eleven] have not been wasted," Brooks wrote. The new author replied immediately that it would take "more than ten years to express" his gratitude to Houghton Mifflin. He knew of course that the publisher's enthusiasm for the novel meant they thought they could make money on it. He liked that side of it too.

They took up the matter of a title, in correspondence. Cooper preferred *The Hills of Sironia,* but *Party Town,* he said, would do. This title could contrast ironically the importance of Sironia's social activity with the ugly, sordid life beneath. He put it in his manuscript this way: "You know what a *party* town Sironia is. Far more talk will be used up on—tonight's affair, for instance, than on the new syrup factory which will increase our weekly pay roll."[4]

That Wild Lie, Tam Lipscomb, and *Harp of a Thousand Strings* were other suggestions by Cooper, which the publishers rejected.

Finding no agreement on a title they let that problem rest while editor Brooks attempted to persuade Cooper to travel to Boston for conferences. Among the issues to settle with the author was publication date. The editor advised against trying to get the big novel on a fall, 1952, list. This would give them only nine months. He pointed out that it would rush the critics who would have only a short time to read it. This would go against the book, he said. This judgment soon bowed to other circumstances.

Brooks baited him further with the news that Cooper would be the twenty-first author to receive the Houghton Mifflin Literary Fellowship Award, then only $2,500. Half of it would be an advance against royalty.

"I am so pleased that should the Texas Power and Light Company's current fail tonight the fact would not be noticed by anyone in my vicinity," Cooper wrote Brooks. During the month that had elapsed since Brooks invited the Waco writer to Boston, Cooper wished more and more to make the trip. He brought up the subject with lawyers Howell and Naman, without detailing why he needed to leave town. He was delighted to learn they had gone far enough in their case preparation to free him for a few days, so he wrote Brooks to expect him in Boston on February 25. Because of his dislike for flying, he would ride the train.

So far not a word had gone from either the writer or the publisher to the press. Brooks suggested that Houghton Mifflin make the first announcement, "Actually the papers do not generally run any extras on the subject, but we like to get all the publicity we can."

Besides getting information for the planned news release, Houghton Mifflin executives wanted to know Cooper better, if they were going to invest over $60,000 in his product.

Among the many people Cooper met in Boston (and he liked them all) was Jack Leggett, H-M's publicity man. Leggett instantly perceived the news value in the situation. That a wealthy, good-looking bachelor of fifty-seven years had written his first novel, soon to be known as the longest ever published in America, was news, particularly when spliced with the fact that the secretly produced novel would be published by one of the most respected publishers in the business. *Time* magazine agreed, and if Houghton and Cooper would sit on the story until the issue dated April 7, *Time* would break the news with good play. Naturally everyone agreed.

XII *Sironia, Texas*

THE *WACO NEWS-TRIBUNE* and *Time* broke the story of Madison Cooper's novel on April 3. *Time's* story struck several discordant notes. One especially would reverberate harshly across the years picking up new errors as it gained credence. This then was the first published statement of the genesis of Cooper's characters: "Waco folks will undoubtedly be looking for themselves and their neighbors among the huge cast of characters. Cooper says they'll have no luck: all of his people are made up." Such a statement in *Time* was the first of many spoken and written erroneous speculations that Cooper's novel was an exposé of his fellow citizens and a rattling of family skeletons. *Time* erred in saying that the novel due from Houghton Mifflin was Cooper's second novel. Not so. His first book-length manuscript was a nonfiction item never published and later destroyed.

The novel still had no name. Cooper had pointed to the trunk where one of three copies of the novel manuscript had been stored. *Time* quoted him, "I've hit my knee and torn my pants on that trunk so many times that I've taken to calling the whole thing just Ugh." Cooper took pains later to tell that *Time* misspelled the last word. It was Ug, a show of pain—not Ugh, implying strong distaste. At any rate the unnamed novel went by the name Ugh or Ug for several weeks.

". . . owns so much real estate that it takes all his time to manage it," said *Time*. The news magazine could not be expected to go into detail on the complications of how the author amassed money, but stopping short as it did led Paul Crume of the *Dallas Morning News* to write that Cooper was a real-estate man. Thus United Press picked up the error and seeded newspapers coast to coast with the word that Cooper was a real-estate operator. And NBC jumped into the comedy of errors with a taped interview saying Cooper was a 27-year-old real-estate agent who had sold a novel to a Houston publishing house.

Publishers' Weekly then noted that another super-length novel was published in England that same year—it was H. F. M. Prescott's *The Man on a Donkey.* Like the projected Cooper book, the Prescott opus was in two volumes. Cooper's 840,000-word book was longer than the Old and New Testaments combined and far longer than *An American Tragedy, Of Time and the River, Gone with the Wind, Raintree County, Anthony Adverse,* and *House Divided. New York Times'* David Dempsey noted that the novel by the Texan was a product of time, not agony. Cooper claimed it was both.

The rush of publicity was on. Waco hadn't had so much national attention in a literary way since pamphleteer William Cowper Brann was assassinated in 1898. *Vogue, Look,* and others followed *Time* in photographing and interviewing the new author. The news service accounts caused comment everywhere as Houghton Mifflin supplied information and photographs from its own publicity department. Here's how the *New York Herald-Tribune* reported the Houghton release:

> Trembling with awe, a bulletin from Boston says Houghton Mifflin is standing guard over what will be the longest American novel ever published—an 840,000 word manuscript, as yet untitled, by Madison A. Cooper, Jr., a Waco, Texas, businessman. It appears that the H-M people find it not only long but good; they have honored Mr. Cooper with their Literary Fellowship. . . .
>
> The previous H-M house record is 1,514 pages—which fitted into one book, but was apt to be dangerous if dropped on a human foot or on one of the smaller domestic animals.
>
> The longest novel ever written in English? The New York Public Library's information bureau declared no final statement was available, but said the consensus of scholarly opinion named Samuel Richardson's *Clarissa Harlowe.* The four unabridged volumes of that work in the Everyman edition total 2,119 pages averaging 400 words each. That would be 847,600 words.

Later someone pointed out that *Clarissa* was originally serialized, which made Cooper's book the longest in history to be published originally in book form.

As the spring shower of publicity turned into a summer downpour, Houghton Mifflin discreetly let it be known that they preferred the publicity abate until they had something to show the public. But such a reaction was the result of a hard choice. It is a maxim in the publishing and entertainment industries that any publicity is better than none. Paul Brooks himself had told Cooper that "we try to get all the publicity we can." Now the Boston people were saying the public would get tired of hearing about the novel before it was published, and Cooper was saying that no novel could live up to the expectations created by the deluge of prepublication attention.

This wide national coverage of a new writer created enough excitement among the staff members of Houghton Mifflin to cause them to set October 22, then November 3, 1952, as publication date. Ignored now were Brooks's early fears that to rush publication would hurt the critical reception. No book in their memory had received this kind of prepublication publicity.

Madison Cooper came to love his new fame. At first, he apologized to friends by saying he didn't like publicity but was going along in gratitude to Houghton Mifflin for their big gamble on his work and because he found the news people likable. Then he began to enjoy it openly. While the press rolled out the Cooper story to news readers, the editorial and sales staff at Houghton Mifflin had important loose ends to tie down. The title, for example.

They considered for a month calling the novel *Tam*. They pondered calling it *The Hackberry Tree*, symbolizing how the new generation replaced the old in the town of Sironia as the hackberry tree overtook the slow-growing, aristocratic magnolia—symbol of the Old South. Although the title *The Hackberry Tree* leaked to a few newspapers as the chosen title, its future was uncertain from the beginning.

The sales force, with the editorial staff, convened to decide:

> Though the book appeared in the preliminary proof bulletin under the title of *The Hackberry Tree,* the sales staff—as well as Lovell, Hardwick, Dorothy, and myself were unanimously in favor of *Sironia, Texas*. So be it. . . . The only practicable solution is two volumes. Price: Probably $10.00

Cooper didn't actually fight the decision on the title, but he had a few words on the subject:

> The selection of title—as always—entirely up to Houghton, but I'd like my reactions to *Sironia, Texas* on file:
> a. It capitalizes on the current interest in Texas.
> b. It is unusual, in that I don't recall a title which included both town and state names.
> c. It does emphasize the book's chief unity, that of location.

d. It ties in with all the UP and AP publicity which has mentioned both Sironia and Texas, sometimes repeatedly.
However,
a. It does not spotlight Tam as the main character.
b. Some will undoubtedly say, "The chief protagonist is a town," which might be confusing, since a number of novels have been weakened, in my estimation, by the reader's not knowing who the head man is. I tried to avoid this by a very early interpolation: ". . . Tam, whose story this chiefly is."
c. It is not a "graphic" title, nor one on which "gags" can be based, thus getting more publicity.

In this letter Cooper failed to mention what he was to repeat many times later—that *Sironia, Texas* put the reader on notice that it was a typically Texas story, thereby giving credence to the legend that it was a story of Waco.

With the title settled, Cooper gave quick second thoughts to the name over which *Sironia, Texas* would appear—Matt Cooper. That's what his oldest friends called him, and some relatives. Furthermore, he had already published under that name. He had reasons upon reasons why Matt was better than Madison, but the publisher considered them unimportant in the face of the well-established Madison Cooper which the public knew by now. Madison Cooper it would be on his books.

Cooper went out of his way to try to convince others that *Sironia, Texas* would be a book that everyone could enjoy. He wrote to an out-of-town bank president, ". . . my book is written for people like you and me—nothing highbrow about it." He hoped, and expected, readers to find *Sironia* warming, *humorous.*

Possibly to protect the common touch of his novel, more likely to avoid being held accountable for views he could not support, Cooper obtained his publisher's agreement not to change a word of the manuscript except with the author's consent. They, of course, had the right to make routine grammatical and spelling corrections. He was proud of this show of confidence from the publisher and recited it occasionally to interested listeners. Regardless of how Cooper took this, it is impossible to consider it a real concession. Brooks and several of his colleagues were skilled in presenting their case for changes and remarkably adroit in working with authors. Cooper once called Brooks the "answer to an author's prayer." Brooks and his fellow toilers could communicate with Cooper convincingly. Although it can't be said he always capitulated gladly, it can be said that he usually gave in gracefully enough.

The question of bowdlerizing *Sironia* is the best case in point. Cooper never denied the book described violence vividly or that the sexual theme came through boldly. However, *Sironia, Texas* has "95 parts warm, human, homely details about likable people" as it has perhaps five parts high-voltage shocks, he said.

Sales and executive departments of the publishing house challenged the advisability of using "nigger" instead of Negro—or colored man, which term Cooper considered a phony euphemism. Cooper quarreled a little about keeping the first spelling, chiefly because it never in his life had occurred to him to hate Negroes. Hence, the word from him bore no condescension. Life in a place like his Sironia depended on the warp of the Negro community being closely woven into the woof of white lives. He knew as well as anyone that 1952 atmosphere was different from the Sironia era. For this reason, he resisted superimposing the racial attitudes of the 1950s on a time past. The agreed result between author and publisher was that if a Sironian were speaking or thinking, he could use "nigger." But if the reader might deduce that it was the author's own word, Negro would be the spelling rule. Few such changes were necessary.

The Boston-Waco bowdlerizing proceeded. But it is important to know that the quantity of rewriting and cutting "with the author's approval" was actually insignificant in a book so long. Cooper rewrote several sentences, and in retrospect the original often makes an intelligible, good-humored point to the reader who can understand Cooper language and intent. The bowdlerized sentence or passage, on the other hand, sometimes makes no sense—unless the reader can guess the words omitted.

"As fine for sales as 'banned in Boston' is said to be, I don't want that variety of publicity," Cooper said not knowing that he was destined to come in for more than his share of it. "I'd hate to see a manuscript as honestly written as I have tried to make this one reduced to 'mush' by removing everything that might offend anybody, reasonable or unreasonable."

The author and others made some ill-conceived remarks to newsmen that came out in print and caused speculation among readers that *Sironia, Texas* was far dirtier in manuscript than in published form.

A latter day survey of the author-publisher correspondence and edited galley proofs shows that Houghton Mifflin suggested only forty-one specific changes in the giant manuscript. The bowdlerizing was aimed chiefly at sex in the conversation of two Sironia teenagers —Tam Lipscomb and Splice Rogan. Other instances occurred in the author's description of Tam's and Charles Storrow's practical introduction to the sex act and a scattered few in other description and dialogue.

About one-third as many references to race and fecal imagery were questioned by the publisher as sex. Anyone who accused Madison Cooper of malice toward Negroes is ignorant of the man and his book, however, the publisher held that he would be so judged because he used the term *nigger* and because he suggested that a long-unbathed Negro had a distinctive odor in warm climate quite different from the smell of an unwashed Caucasian.

Publication of H-M's important novel was still four months away when reports of advance sales to bookstores indicated that *Sironia, Texas* would be a bestseller. H-M salesmen were making good use of the prepublication publicity. Orders were coming for quantity lots.

XIII The Long Novel Dies

LITERARY GOSSIPS IN New York City in midsummer 1952 loved spreading the latest leak—that *Sironia, Texas* would not be for the kiddies or the Bible Belt. In Waco, someone unaware of Madison Cooper's secret literary labors spanning nearly thirty-five years, referred to the impending novel publication as "another of his eccentricities." The remark went straight to him on the gossip network. He thought it flattery and passed it on to a friend saying that modern dictionaries were being rewritten to define "eccentric as 'whatever the speaker is not.' " It's no secret that this man cultivated not only a reputation as a gossip to learn what people cover up; he cultivated the legend of his eccentricity as well. If he were eccentric, such eccentricity in reality was colorless compared with the thrilling hearsay still making the rounds in Waco many years after his death. Instead of being bothered by what people thought, he amplified the Cooper legend in Waco because it gave him the freedom to behave as he pleased. At center he was a ruthlessly well-organized and self-disciplined man. Cooper's twentieth-century Calvinistic morals underlay his approach to life. Usually he was a nonconforming ascetic.

When put to the test, however, as during this time of newly found fame, Cooper proved he could perform in the role of conscientious conformist. He bought a Brooks Brothers suit in New York, calling it his autographing suit, and determined to autograph books and exchange compliments with bookstore personnel and customers as a new author should. He would even appear on television, provided the interviewer avoided political and other controversial questions, and provided the interviewer spoke near his right ear. He would even agreeably sit through dull speeches.

When the Sironia year arrived, Cooper understood his contemporaries so well—as individuals—that he could project his consciousness into thoughts of other men, and women, and children. In a practical sense he could see through most people and virtually read their minds. This very characteristic in the author, this confluence of perception, vigor, and experience would strike readers of *Sironia,*

Texas which sold so fast before publication that for a month after publication day Houghton Mifflin had no books to fill new orders from bookstores. The publisher reported it was out of stock until December when 25,000 copies of *Sironia* were in print.

Cooper and his novel, touted so abundantly for months in advance, rapidly fell victim to superficial ballyhoo. Newspapers, magazines, radio and television programs had scattered the superficial facts and errors across the nation. Such information set fixed ideas in many minds before reviewers and readers had a chance to assess and report on the depth of the book.

Some readers quailed at the length; others shied at the $10 price tag. Influential Virginia Kirkus told bookstores and libraries no book is good enough to be that long.

Skeptics could not believe a businessman could produce first-rate prose, especially in a first novel. So, they asked, what does the book have to deserve the publicity? The real answer appeared in the circumstances surrounding the book's publication, that is, the true news value of Cooper as an unusual individual. Then there was the ingredient of a myth in Houghton Mifflin's buying an 840,000-word manuscript over the transom. *Sironia* made its way alone and unaided. The publishing house saw it as a gripping story, a good novel that would sell—every publisher's dream.

The cocktail party critics could not know all the background, so they cast about for an easy answer. Since it was easy to deduce *Sironia's* interest hinged on sensationalism, they quickly settled for that. Then when the book fell into their hands, they looked for sex and violence to justify their guess. Finding some of both, they brushed off the book—satisfied with their perspicacity. Many didn't bother to read it.

The unprecedented prepublication publicity indirectly hurt the book exactly as Brooks predicted months earlier. He counseled against rushing the literary critics to read the long book, but the sales force later overruled him. Reviewers had the equivalent of seven or eight novels to read and assess in six weeks or less, if they attempted to publish their views while timely. A selected few influential reviewers received the book earlier in bound galley proofs, a poor presentation of a book at best. Errors in many reviews indicate the book went largely unread by critics. Other reviews only rehashed the publisher's jacket blurb and the old news angles. Only the conscientious reviewers read the whole book and gave honest assessments to their readers.

Novels had been in a steady decline as popular entertainment since the end of World War II when the nonfiction book and television edged into America's inner mind. In 1952 novels experienced a brief revival to their old glory. Part of the credit must go to Houghton Mifflin and its blockbuster.

Sironia ran in fast company that season.

Scribner's in October, 1952, provided the public with Ernest Hemingway's novella, *The Old Man and the Sea. Life* magazine serialized it immediately. About the same time Viking Press brought out *East of Eden,* a hefty novel by John Steinbeck. His story was long, stretched in time from the Civil War to World War I, and covered the nation geographically from Connecticut to Salinas Valley, California.

And Doubleday gave the public *Giant* by Edna Ferber. Her caricature of Texans stirred controversy in this state that eclipsed much of *Sironia's* impact. Early in the year the Macmillan Company provided its own outsized novel, Miss H. F. M. Prescott's *The Man on the Donkey.*

Nor was that the end of it. Although a handsome production, *Sironia* was on the nation's bookshelves at $10 retail, cheek by jowl with Hemingway's *Old Man* selling for $3, Steinbeck's *East of Eden* for $4.50, Ferber's *Giant* for $3.95, and the Prescott book for $5. These notable publishing products, of course, were not alone in competing for the place sought by *Sironia, Texas.* American publishing houses delivered a total of twelve thousand new titles in 1952 trade books. About 2,100 were novels.

Sironia wasn't beaten hands down. Conditionally, the novel found amazing success. Sales for two months soared through four printings to about 23,000 pairs of volumes. The $10 trade edition had a gilded sister in the $15 version called a Texas edition. *Sironia, Texas* joined the new works of Hemingway, Steinbeck, and Ferber on bestseller lists. The *New York Times* book section gave the big novel a full page front cover review. This pleased Cooper as much as any single result of publication. And it helped account for the fact that *Sironia* sold twice as many copies as any other American novel had done at $10. Cooper's royalties with the $1,200 outright fellowship grant, amounted to nearly $30,000 for the U.S. publication alone.

Franz J. Horch of New York City eagerly sought publication rights for Neilsen, Presses de la Cité in France. However, the French publisher would have to cut the book, he said, claiming no European publisher could afford to publish such a long novel.

Brooks immediately wrote Cooper of this European publishing possibility, and recommended that Cooper approve it. Cooper said no in characteristic style on December 16, 1952:

> If *Sironia, Texas* is outstanding or exceptional in any way, it is in the feeling of "Audience Participation" a sympathetic reading engenders in its happenings. This is due largely to the almost limitless detail, which reviewers who weren't willing to, or couldn't, give the book the necessary careful reading never got into its spirit. As a result they got from it nothing more than a series of sensational incidents, i.e., the portions they did read carefully, spaced by what they took to be padding.
>
> Allowed to cut *Sironia* as they see fit, clients of the Franz J. Horch Agency would almost certainly pursue one of two methods: (1) Reduce the whole book to a lifeless synopsis; or (2) omit the portions which give the book meaning I sought, go-to-town with the sensational and shocking parts (included by me only to make the whole thing credible) and end up with another Duchess Hotpants sort of THING. . . .
>
> Most assuredly I do not say I won't approve any translation-plan; might even O.K. one for dividing the ms. into a number of shorter books, for simultaneous or widely spaced publication. But (for the present anyway) I am not willing for its text to be cut in any way for translation or other purpose.

Soon afterwards a Danish publisher came forward with an offer to publish the entire novel in eight separate volumes. It would sell in three formats at $14, $20, and $27 per set. It went into a second edition in 1961 of 5,000 sets of eight volumes each. The first edition ran 3.000 sets of eight.

But in the United States the book quickly breathed its last. Of the total of 25,000 copies printed, about 23,000 sold during the first two months after publication. Sales dried up in early 1953 and by midyear Houghton Mifflin found itself with over 2,000 copies on hand, a few returns, and no prospect of disposing of them handily. Hardwick Moseley told Cooper at this point that H-M would like to try an experiment in San Francisco where *Sironia* had a big booster who would promote the book if he could cut the price to $5.95 per set. This would reduce Cooper's royalty but promote his reputation, Moseley said. Cooper countered with the idea of changing the dust jackets and selling the books for $4.50 each. A stalemate resulted.

And *Sironia, Texas* was the same as dead.

Movie interest, once very hot while publisher and author remained cool and overconfident, never revived to the point of a lucrative offer. *East of Eden, Old Man and the Sea,* and *Giant* garnered the existing big movie sales of that year.

No record of a suit, or threat of suit, over *Sironia, Texas* is recorded. It is a matter of record that *Sironia* was smeared by the Waco far-right hate press. It is also a matter of record that a Boston censor branded it as Not Recommended in a black list called "Books on Trial." It was joined in this list by books authored by Joyce Cary, Aldous Huxley, and John Howard Griffin, among others.

Some readers hailed *Sironia, Texas* as a social document of lasting value; others called it a magnificent story. Many drew parallels between people they knew during the first two decades of the twentieth century, and counterparts in Sironia.

Sironia made money for the publisher and author and thereby made connections for Cooper which he tried to exploit with another novel—much shorter—turned out in less than two years, named *The Haunted Hacienda.* He intended it to be the first of three volumes to be published separately. Houghton Mifflin exploited the prepublication processes to establish itself as boss in the Cooper-H-M Co. relationship. True to form, Cooper countered with his own self-assertions. It was then that the old exchange of affection and enthusiasm appeared to freeze on both sides.

Strange, original, occasionally vulgar, and full of life, said someone writing of *The Haunted Hacienda.* The same individual in the next breath said the book had some good writing, that the Molly Bailey circus episode was unequaled anywhere, that Guido was different from Tam—a good sign in a writer. The book came out in 1955, but with none of the excitement bred by *Sironia.*

XIV Community Gifts

COOPER RECEIVED THE McMurray Bookshop Award for 1952's best first novel by a Texan. He immediately channeled the money into a special fund for needy writers, but it drew no further contributions as he hoped it would. Frank Dobie later suggested that Cooper himself add to it; officious suggestion, the donor thought. Later the McMurray award money ended up in operating funds of the Texas Institute of Letters of which Cooper was a council member.

Fame did not diminish his impulse to offer financial aid when he saw a need. During a 1955 visit to New York, Cooper listened to a journalist describe his uncertain future. He had left a well-known national news magazine with no job in sight. Cooper confounded the man by offering financial help "in the event of need." By letter the journalist declined the offer and described his reactions: "This is precisely the rarest reaction [Cooper's offer] that someone out of a job ever encounters. Nothing of the sort has ever occurred to me before and I have never heard of it happening to anyone else in New York publishing and literary circles."

To sketch in the variety of his charitable and educational gifts during the four and one-half years when the public knew he was a writer, the list below notes all contributions Cooper made personally. These are typical of the gifts he made increasingly from the mid-1930s onward. (Gifts from Madison Cooper *personally* do not cover Cooper Foundation grants.)

1952:
First Presbyterian Church, Waco Community Chest, Crippled Children's Hospital in Waco, American Red Cross, Boy Scout Building Fund, National Recreation Association, Providence Hospital, and a $10,029.09 donation to Cooper Foundation. The Providence gift was $6,000 to remodel and equip a ward (Miriam Hall) for psychiatric patients, the first facility of its kind in Waco.

1953:

First Presbyterian Church, Waco United Fund (taking the place of the Community Chest), Catholic High School funds, Waco Disaster Relief Fund (tornado), Waco Civic Theater Building Fund, Association for the Blind in Waco, and Muscular Dystrophy Association. The Civic Theater, tornado victims, and United Fund received $8,000, $5,000, and $3,000 respectively.

1954:

Sigma Alpha Epsilon Student Aid Fund, Cooper Foundation, March of Dimes, McLennan County Association for the Blind, Boy Scout Building Fund, Waco United Fund, Muscular Dystrophy Association, First Presbyterian Church, Paul Quinn College, and Providence Hospital. Cooper Foundation received the $12,401.99 lion's share. United Fund was next at $3,000.

1955:

March of Dimes, First Presbyterian Church, Waco United Fund, one year's salary for McLennan County's first woman probation officer, St. Stephen's Episcopal School in Austin, Red Cross Eastern Flood Relief, SAE Educational Building Fund, and Cooper Foundation.

1956:

Conference of Southwest Foundations, Texas Presbyterian "Together for Christ Campaign," Waco State Home Independent School District (for 16 and 35 mm movie equipment), March of Dimes, Junior Chamber of Commerce of Crockett, SAE Alumni Association, and Waco United Fund.

Death cut short further gifts in 1956. One of the 1956 contributions adds pieces to the Cooper mosaic: the Crockett, Texas, Junior Chamber of Commerce received Cooper funds to help pay college expenses for one year of study for a Negro girl handicapped since birth. She could use neither her arms nor her legs, but the Texas Education Agency considered her a brilliant girl who would make a fine speech therapist. Law prohibited the agency's paying all her college expenses; she had no money of her own; and word reached Cooper. He provided the necessary additional funds and indicated he might come through again the second year if she could make a go of college work.

Relentlessly close with the exact amount of money he dispensed, he distributed so many small gifts that in retrospect he appears lavish.

He saved his best gift for the people of Waco. Madison Cooper was never the Tam Lipscomb of Sironia, but it was Tam who learned a lesson from his fictional father, Marshall: "Nobody worth his salt ever hates his home." Waco was Cooper's home; he was a product of it. He loved it.

"I was born, raised, and hope to die in Waco, Texas," he wrote proudly.

XV The Last Mile

ALTHOUGH AT LEAST one perceptive man believed Cooper never looked well after the ill-fated *The Haunted Hacienda* publication in 1955, most people who knew Madison Cooper had no inkling that September 28, 1956, would see the end of this lonely man.

Two days earlier, Cooper's nephew, Lawrence C. Lacy, received a characteristically good-humored note addressed to Lacy's newly arrived daughter. Cooper sent a U.S. Savings Bond to his new great-niece, and supplied her with her first nickname. To Golda Rixon Lacy, Cooper typed:

Dear Ricky Lacy,
    Your being late is being overlooked this time, but don't let it happen again.
    It is hoped that you will be lastingly grateful to your mother for all she went through in getting you here and to your father, too, for whatever it was he did.
                                        M.A.C.

Then came the last afternoon at the track.

Chinaberry and hackberry trees dot the small park areas at the corners of Waco Municipal Stadium—once the site of all important football games in Waco, including Baylor University games. The stadium is on the old Texas Cotton Palace grounds, about where the exposition's race track used to resound to thundering hooves. Muny Stadium consists of wooden bleachers rising high on both sides of its Bermuda grass-turfed football field. A red cinder track circles the playing field.

For a long time Madison Cooper had had a key to the lock on the northeast gate.

This afternoon of September 28 was muggy, so warm and humid that Mary Farrell remembers walking onto her front porch across town and thinking, "How can anyone live in this heat!" She never thought of the words as prophetic. They only expressed her discomfort. The whole Southwest had been in a long drought, the worst in fifty years.

At Muny Stadium sixty-three-year-old Madison Cooper stopped his old Packard on the parking lot at the north end of the stadium. The automobile was parallel with a cement sidewalk poured years ago during the Cotton Palace era to accommodate foot traffic along the back of the racing stables. In 1956 such sidewalks were virtually all that was left of the once world-renowned exposition that had its heyday during the same years as the Cooper Grocery Company. Ordinarily, Cooper would have parked at the northeast gate or driven inside the fence close to the dressing room where he changed into a sweat suit. But tonight there would be a football game. If he parked at the gate or inside, his car would be in the way of early arriving official vehicular traffic en route to the dressing room or small ticket office. He didn't want to get involved or be slowed getting out.

Wearing tennis shoes, woolen socks, a pair of worn khaki trousers, white dress shirt under a plaid cotton flannel shirt, Cooper let himself in the gate and followed the familiar path to the dressing room.

J. L. Mayfield, a stadium caretaker, glanced at him only casually as Cooper ran his laps—the same exercise he had taken (weather permitting) three times weekly for many years. Mayfield had worked there several years and had seen Cooper hundreds of times. Cooper always gave Christmas gifts to the stadium caretakers and game attendants. Mayfield noticed Cooper about to leave the field. He thinks this was about five o'clock.

"Well, I'll see you next week," Mayfield heard Cooper say. "I think you've got too much water on the field tonight." The day was Friday, and high-school football was in high gear on another fall football schedule. Field preparations were for the game between Waco High School and Woodrow Wilson High School of Dallas. Cooper headed for his parked automobile. No one noticed him when he opened the car door and seated himself behind the steering wheel. There was no eye witness to the movements or the minutes that elapsed as he started his automobile engine and fell against the left door, then forward, resting against the steering wheel.

Mr. and Mrs. Herb Wise arrived to open the stadium's two ticket offices. Mrs. Wise handled the South Fifteenth Street office. Big, friendly, and husky-voiced Wise worked on a smaller but busy structure near the northeast gate. They had business to attend to, and a car on the parking lot on game night was to be expected. Police Capt. Tom Bennett, who would work the game, drove up to the northeast gate in his radio patrol car about six. He was early for an eight o'clock game.

Albert Fortune moonlighted as a stadium attendant—his job was to stand guard at the dressing room to keep unauthorized visitors out. Fortune, from his home across South Fifteenth Street, saw other cars gathering on the parking lot and told himself it was time to get to the stadium. He thinks it was about ten minutes past six when he strode down the sidewalk on his way to the northeast gate. In later years he could have cut diagonally across from his home to the gate and would have missed the Packard on the parking lot. But in 1956 the area between the stadium's north end and the parking lot was grown up in trees and shrubs to obstruct a free view of the stadium games. Fortune, one of the attendants who had received gifts from Madison Cooper, recognized the car as he approached it. He saw no one inside.

"When I passed along the sidewalk in front of the car, I could tell the motor had been running a long time because it was hot."

A few steps farther and "I could see the exhaust still coming out so I knew it was still running."

Fortune might have reached inside the window on the driver's side to turn off the ignition switch, but the window was rolled up. He opened the door to cut the motor and the author's body almost tumbled from the car.

Fortune caught it in his arms and laid the limp form down on the seat to the right. He turned off the ignition switch and ran a few yards toward the gate, shouting to Captain Bennett and Mr. Wise to call an ambulance. Something was wrong with Mr. Cooper.

"I thought when I opened the door that he had just passed out, or maybe fainted," Fortune said later. But a second look told him it was all over. Another patrol car soon arrived and the police kept a crowd from gathering.

At Cooper's home Bertha had dinner ready and was worried. She had worked for the family a long time and knew Madison Cooper's clock-dominated habits. She called Brad Hoover and no one answered. Then she telephoned Lawrence Lacy.

"Something bad must have happened to Mr. Madison." Her words to Lacy were rushed and tense.

"He's off his schedule." She offered this as clear proof that something was wrong. His unvarying practice was to come home from the track in time to bathe and dress before his evening meal at 6:30.

Lacy agreed with Bertha that it was unusual, but it could be car trouble—a hundred things. He tried to comfort Bertha who was genuinely frightened. A few minutes later Lawrence Lacy drove out of his own driveway taking his two older children with him on an errand and heard an ambulance siren nearing Providence Hospital down the street. He pushed the idea out of his mind that it might be his celebrated uncle, but he still wanted reassurance that all was well, so he headed toward 1801 Austin Avenue.

Bertha was distraught. She knew nothing of the events of the past hour and a half, but dinner was getting cold and Mr. Madison still wasn't at home. Yielding to his first impulse, Lawrence turned his car toward the Catholic hospital. Upon arriving, he found his brother Roane and their mother, Cooper's sister Lucile. Roane had already made the identification.

Cooper's relatives naturally proceeded with preliminary funeral arrangements, but they were fully aware of the increasingly important role assumed in recent years by R. B. Hoover and the Cooper Foundation. Roane Lacy called Hoover whom Cooper had been quietly grooming to take over as executive secretary of the foundation. The Hoover family knew nothing of the evening's events. They had been out to eat at a restaurant with plans to attend the Waco High School football game that evening. En route to Muny Stadium they paused at their home. The telephone was ringing when the family car rolled up on the driveway. It was Roane Lacy. From the telephone Hoover passed quickly to his desk where he reached for a plain white business-size envelope. It was sealed, resealed with cellophane tape, and triple sealed with three strips of plain brown manila gummed tape. Typed across the front:

PERSONAL PROPERTY OF MADISON A. COOPER, JR. In case of whose death this envelope is to be opened only by his property manager at the time of his death.

Hoover broke open the envelope and read for the first time:

Between the time of my death and the time my executor can take charge of my Estate, which should be only a day or two at most, preferably only a few hours, you are to act as my personal repre-

sentative with full charge of my Estate except that no change of
ownership of any part thereof can be effected and no disbursement
or distribution of same be made, or liability therefor incurred.

From that moment every detail of the funeral arrangements, disposi-
tion of personal effects, management of the estate, dealing with the
executor and the public, and the course to be taken by his Cooper
Foundation would be carried out according to a detailed plan devised
by Madison Cooper himself, beginning with funeral instructions
drawn up in 1947. Hoover and Hilton E. Howell, vice-chairman of
the foundation, assumed the responsibility of putting Cooper's wishes
into effect.

The next morning Dr. K. P. Wittstruck, pathologist, determined
by autopsy that cause of death was acute heart failure associated
with marked pulmonary congestion and edema. This was secondary
to acute coronary insufficiency. There was moderate coronary arterio-
sclerosis, but no apparent coronary thrombosis commonly associated
with an acute "heart attack." Justice of the Peace Vic Hall, following
consultation with H. E. Howell, ordered the post-mortem examination
for at least three reasons: Cooper was alone at death, he had shown
no signs of illness, and he had not been under the care of a physician
immediately before. Further, Cooper's position in the city where he
lived required a proper public explanation of the cause of death.

The funeral went according to Madison Cooper's written orders:
Dressed in a dark business suit (not the autographing one from
Brooks Brothers), his body was wrapped in two army blankets from
the chifforobe in his bedroom and placed in a wooden coffin box
for burial. Also according to his written instructions, there was no
service at the funeral home, only a simple and brief service at the
Cooper plot in Oakwood Cemetery. Cooper's loyalty to his childhood
pastor, the Rev. C. T. Caldwell, came out once more in his request
that, if possible, the Rev. Mr. Caldwell officiate at the burial. The
old man's eyesight failing, he recited Bible verses from memory as
he conducted the service. The mourners stood in the hot sun-dappled
shade around the burial plot. His instructions said he wanted no
flowers, but the word did not reach everyone.

There was one place left on the Cooper plot before the angel for
a grave—between Madison's mother and father.

Simple headstones of like design mark each grave—father, son,
mother, and sister Christine who died the year the son was born.

Epilogue

WITH THE BRIEF funeral behind them, the men entrusted with direction of the Cooper Foundation and the Madison Cooper estate turned to the well-charted future devised during the preceding thirteen years.

"I have purposely arranged to make payments while I am living to all my former beneficiaries except Cooper Foundation, so that said foundation can be my sole beneficiary under my will," he had written over three years earlier. These words and thousands more were among the several memoranda in the triple-sealed envelope left in the care of R. B. Hoover.

Another typed page labeled "Supplemental Instructions to Trustees of Cooper Foundation, to Accompany my Last Will and Testament," established Madison Cooper's wishes for use of his home of forty-nine years:

> My home at 1801 Austin . . . is to be used as headquarters for the foundation, or, if the trustees prefer, the home may be wrecked and the ground rented on long-term lease. I do not want the home, as it is, rented for any purpose.

In a later memorandum left with Hoover, Cooper amplified the future of the old home:

> If PRACTICABLE (in trustees' opinion) I would like my home at 1801 Austin Avenue . . . to become not only the headquarters of Cooper Foundation, but a civic center, a source of practical instruction and cultural improvement.[1]
>
> However, if the trustees think it better to give a long-term lease on this property or handle it in other ways, there is nothing to prevent same, so long as ownership of same is retained.

Still further, he wrote:

> . . . it may be that it will be better to wreck the old home and get a

ground lease on the lots. Under no circumstances, do I want it leased
as a residence to anyone, although I have no objection to the (foundation executive director) living in part of it if that seems a good idea.

Neither foundation trustees nor anyone else was apprised before
his death of the total contents of 1801 Austin Avenue, and the
house stood empty until remodeling made the second floor suitable
for offices of Cooper Foundation. Public curiosity excited by the
sudden death of the secretive author-millionaire brought out hundreds
of visitors who contented themselves with passing by the house in
their automobiles. Others, emboldened by the absence of the owner,
looked for souvenirs in the garden and exterior of the house. Such
uninvited attention naturally frightened Bertha who was living in the
garage apartment at the rear of the main house. So this combination
of circumstances brought the foundation officials to post an around-
the-clock police guard at the residence for ten days after the funeral,
briefly and inadvertently compounding the erroneous belief that the
structure housed items of great value, or dark secrets.

Madison Cooper's will conveying his personal estate, estimated in
1956 to be worth over three million dollars, had rested in a safety
deposit box at the First National Bank of Waco for three years.
Brought to light, it directed the executor to quickly settle any claims
against the estate and transfer the properties to the Cooper Foundation, the irrevocable benevolent trust which is to administer the estate
forever as part of its corpus. The will contained his hope "that in
the years following my death many thousands of Texans will benefit
through the legacy hereinafter authorized."

Item Six of the will again noted his concern over the reputation
of the Cooper Foundation: "To counteract further baseless insinua-
tions to the effect that I founded Cooper Foundation as a 'tax dodge
for the family,' it is my wish that prior to the year A.D. 2000 no known
relative of mine, by blood or marriage, ever become a trustee of
Cooper Foundation."

Madison Cooper further instructed that no real estate (under any
avoidable circumstances) should be sold or otherwise disposed of
permanently; all property except securities should be directly ad-
ministered by the foundation; all personal belongings not useful to
the Cooper Foundation should be donated to Providence Hospital
of Waco; his business files should be kept at least five years or
longer, depending on their usefulness to the foundation; and his

literary files "(i.e. my writings which have never been completed and which at this time are in the trunk of my attic office; in two of the drawers in the left side of the chifforobe in my bedroom; and in various boxes, trunks, etc. in the attic of my home) are to be destroyed unread and unexamined." Another note indicated that a part of the so-called literary file consisted in part of copious notes gathered in research for the proposed second and third volumes to follow *The Haunted Hacienda,* first volume of a planned trilogy.

"My personal files—at this time in two lower drawers of the walnut-colored metal file cabinet in my bedroom—are to be destroyed. I have recently gone through them and eliminated everything which might embarrass any of my many women friends through the years." Brad Hoover's station wagon made seven fully laden trips to the city incinerator to comply with the file-burning instructions.

Remaining were papers Madison Cooper denoted "permanent files"—hundreds of letters, clippings, documents, miscellaneous manuscript items, materials used in research and organization of *Sironia, Texas* and *The Haunted Hacienda,* memoranda on his literary career, and a complete collection of papers on the Cooper Company, Inc., and long civil suits amassed over a period of sixteen years. Scrapbooks and memorabilia of his early life were also left as property of the Cooper Foundation, as were foundation records.

He prescribed that a "New York City investment house or houses" of foundation trustees' choosing should administer his securities which constituted the bulk of his estate. And he excused educational loans of eight students then in his debt. Upon notification that the remainder of their indebtedness to Madison Cooper was marked paid in full, three of the students wrote their gratitude to the foundation.

Had the Cooper Foundation trustees at the time (1956) declined to accept the estate, Madison Cooper's will provided that a substitute beneficiary would be the University of Texas in Austin. Trustees Howell, Goddard, Boynton, E. N. Dennard, Dr. Lloyd Russell, and William H. Smith accepted the bequest for Waco.

Firm instructions left to the trustees about the possibility that his will might be contested were never put to use.

The trustees employed Cooper's cook as "caretaker" of 1801 Austin, thereby ratifying a contract existing between Mrs. Bertha Lee Walton and the foundation since 1953, and they proceeded as suggested by Madison Cooper to appoint Hoover executive secretary (later executive director). Hilton E. Howell, vice-chairman under

Cooper's aegis, was elected chairman of the board for the first of several five-year terms he would serve. He died in 1968.

Madison Cooper's foundation, an *operating family foundation,* follows his edicts:

> As I think I have made plain frequently, I want Cooper Foundation to be an active living part of the City of Waco in its development along all beneficial lines, functional as well as cultural.
>
> I hope sincerely you [trustees] will do all in your power to make Cooper Foundation the great power for constructive good it can be in our community, and guard its good name carefully.

Perhaps the most salient fact about the Cooper Foundation is Madison Cooper's characteristic juxtaposition of the structure of a *family foundation* over the usual purposes of a *community foundation* which receives many donations for use within a city. Whereas most family foundations are closely restricted as to expenditure of their funds—always carrying out the special interests of the founder—the Cooper Foundation is confined, yet unconfined. Its province is a microcosm of mankind, Waco. Within the framework of their own policies and the trust indenture, the trustees may fund any complete project within the foundation's means that they consider beneficial to Waco. The Cooper Foundation is prohibited from making annual contributions or yearly maintenance assistance.

To carry out its purpose, the foundation grants monies to fill capital needs, to fund innovation or experiment, to sustain pilot and demonstration projects, to provide seed money, and to support first-year expenses incurred by a new community organization needing a chance to prove itself.

When the twenty-fifth year of Cooper Foundation ended, grants could be categorized as follows in order of total contributions: (1) recreation, (2) education, (3) cultural support, (4) help to existing agencies and organizations adjusting to change, (5) health and medical care, (6) welfare, (7) city beautification, (8) public safety, (9) to boost Waco's primary income, (10) to assist Waco as it adjusts to problems of urban growth. Total Cooper Foundation expenditures on more than one hundred and sixty-three grants passed $1.2 million in 1971. Categories often overlap, causing some grants to be as well suited for one category as another. Such multiple purposes are no accident, as the foundation often makes grants it hopes will stimulate additional public effort and continued growth. Like all foundation boards, the Cooper Foundation's directors look for grants likely to have multiplier effect.

Among secondary purposes the foundation seeks is the goal to help Waco reidentify itself in the public mind, i.e., change its image.

The foundation prefers to make grants to organizations which cannot get help elsewhere, to organizations with plans promising success, and to organizations with projects not duplicated by existing agencies and institutions.

Several categories listed above were established during the thirteen years of Madison A. Cooper, Jr.'s foundation chairmanship. Here is an alphabetical listing of categories of Madison Cooper's personal gifts over $5,000 combined with foundation grants made during his lifetime: (1) change, help existing agencies and institutions adjust to, (2) cultural support, (3) education, (4) health, (5) public safety, (6) recreation, (7) welfare. Arrangement of these categories according to total funds contributed cannot be interpreted as meaningful of Madison Cooper's wishes for later foundation grants. To illustrate this point, consider that he donated over $223,000 in property and cash to educational and welfare needs, but in a few years about $200,000 of this total was returned and he made no effort to fill the deficiency created thereby; also his public safety expenditures in another list of gifts would exceed his contributions to recreation, chiefly because the Waco tornado occurring in 1953 led Madison Cooper to contribute $11,050 to the Waco weather station for installation of a radar storm-warning unit. Neither the alphabetical listing, nor arrangement according to total gifts over $5,000 would reflect his annual contributions to the United Fund and other social and welfare needs. Further, the thoughtful person will remember that Madison Cooper responded to community deficiencies as he saw them in the context of his times.

Times change for many reasons, not the least of which is the salubrious effect his Cooper Foundation has had on the quality of Waco urban life. Waco in the lean early days of the Cooper Foundation had no Goodwill Industries, Better Business Bureau, separate jail quarters for youthful offenders, adequate county probation officers, police lie detectors, insecticide fogging apparatus for the city-county health unit, City of Waco library facilities beyond the central building, radium bank for cancer treatment, Legal Aid Clinic, Civil Defense operation, and other basic community facilities that the Cooper Foundation would *help* provide during his lifetime alone.

Numerous other community needs have since been provided by groups of private citizens, McLennan County, the City of Waco, state and federal governments. Problems of urban environment as later conceived had barely begun to be articulated in the Waco he knew. There is no doubt that one of his most far-reaching gifts was to underwrite the rewriting of the Waco city charter. This gift was paid out soon after Madison Cooper's death by his executor, hence it is not listed among foundation grants. The changes in Waco made possible by broadening Waco's city government are virtually incalculable. He did not live to see the Public Administration Services survey of city operations funded by the foundation, although such a survey had his approval. He would never know of the long-range changes in local health, recreation, and welfare programs to result from the *Comprehensive Survey of Human Resources* made by John G. Steinle and Associates in 1959.

Towering above all other changes in the Waco civic climate to come after Madison Cooper's death is the quiet effect of his words, "to make Waco, Texas, a better or more desirable place in which to live." They have become a rule of thumb of thousands of Wacoans; a large share of the credit must go to Madison Cooper.

The Cooper Foundation in 1971 continues to address itself to the quality of the Waco life. Its aim is to avoid assuming any unseemly civic proportions,[2] while helping Waco come to grips with its needs.

NOTES

CHAPTER I

1. Letter from Madison A. Cooper, Jr., to Mrs. Frederick Lewis Allen of New York City, 14 February 1954.

2. Information in August and September, 1925, letters to Ed C. Barrett of Waco, Mrs. Brelsford of Eastland, and Mr. and Mrs. G. C. Walker of San Antonio.

CHAPTER IV

1. Letter from Madison A. Cooper, Jr., to Mrs. John D. Cooper, Jr., of Henderson, N.C., 9 January 1953: "When *Look's* man first hit town, he tried to catch me off base with a sudden 'Why haven't you married?' I answered him, in substance, as follows: 'The first twenty-eight years of my life I had things so exactly my way that I didn't want to settle down, and don't think anyone else in his right mind would have. The next few years—after twenty-eight—I was in love and on the brink of matrimony so many times I wouldn't be positive as to which was the brink-est.' "

2. Letter from C. H. Bell of Houston to Madison A. Cooper, Jr., 30 May 1953.

3. Letter from Madison A. Cooper, Jr., to Jack Leggett of Boston, Mass., 2 May 1952.

4. Letter from Madison A. Cooper, Jr., to Roger N. Conger, 13 December 1929, in Conger Collection, 5854 Mount Rockwood, Waco.

CHAPTER V

1. Letter from Edward Hodnett of Dow Corning Corporation, Midland, Michigan, to Marion Travis, 14 June 1966.

2. Madison Cooper, "My Town: Sironia, Texas," *Writer's Digest,* March 1953, p. 21.

3. Boyden Sparkes (1890-1954) wrote biographical, and collaborated on autobiographical, books on such well-known figures as Walter P. Crysler, M. L. Mellon, Alfred P. Sloan, Jr., Frank Woolworth, Louis J. Horowitz, Henri Carpentier, and Hetty Green.

4. Letter from Boyden Sparkes of New York City to Madison A. Cooper, Jr., 5 December 1952. Note: W. C. Brann was a firebrand pamphleteer in

Waco whose searing invective brought on his murder in 1898. See Charles
Carver, *Brann and the Iconoclast,* (Austin: The University of Texas Press,
1957).

5. Letter from Mack Gorham of New York City to Marion Travis, 2
May 1966.

6. Letter from Madison A. Cooper, Jr., to Jean Wick of New York City,
3 December 1937.

7. Letter from Mrs. Mary Lou Curry Simpson of Silver Springs, Md., to
Madison A. Cooper, Jr., 12 May 1953.

8. Published in Yellow Springs, Ohio, by the Antioch Press, December 1939,
pp. 26–32.

CHAPTER VI

1. Madison Cooper's notes describing biographies of *Sironia, Texas* characters, 1940–1951, Cooper Foundation collection, 1801 Austin Avenue, Waco.

2. U.S. Army in Washington mailed this letter immediately to the San Antonio Procurement District, 24 August 1942.

3. Letter from Lt. Col. Paul H. Brown of San Antonio Officer Procurement
District, Eighth Service Command, 1101 Smith-Young Tower, San Antonio,
to Madison A. Cooper, Jr., 3 September 1942.

4. Letter from Madison Cooper, Jr., to W. R. Poage, House of Represen-
tatives, Washington, D.C., 9 March 1943.

CHAPTER VII

1. Evidence that Madison Cooper cultivated the legend that he was excessively frugal is abundant in the Madison A. Cooper, Jr., papers owned by
Cooper Foundation, 1801 Austin Avenue, Waco, Texas. Consider the following illustrations:

Memorandum for the Cooper Company, Inc., officials on the subject of
labor strikes, 3 December 1946: "As a pennypincher of great renown, I think
I am in a position to counsel that times of 'girding' for the next bout are no
times for penny-pinching by the company."

Letter from Madison A. Cooper, Jr., to Austin Olney of Boston, Mass.,
8 May 1952: "Feel perfectly free to call me 'parsimonious' at any time, as
that is about the only synonym for the same thing I haven't been termed, and
I find the change refreshing."

Letter from Madison A. Cooper, Jr., to Mrs. John D. Cooper of Henderson, North Carolina, 30 April 1952: "You are dead right about my having
inherited my full share of the fine old Cooper 'Scotch,' and have long grown
used to [it]."

2. Interview with Hilton E. Howell, 17 February 1965.

3. Cooper Foundation minute book number one, 7 September 1943.

4. Ibid., p. 7.

CHAPTER VIII

1. Madison Cooper, *Sironia, Texas* (Boston: Houghton Mifflin Co., 1952), 1:48.

2. Ibid., p. 66.

3. Ibid., pp. 479–80.

4. Ibid., pp. 793–94.

5. Ibid., 2:1444.

6. Information from Madison A. Cooper, Jr., to Jack Leggett of Boston, 25 February 1952. Here he listed these preferences: business procedure, the theater, good food, current fiction and nonfiction, small groups of friends, five-ten mile hikes, museums, fairs, and exhibitions.

7. Cooper, *Sironia, Texas,* 1:287.

8. Ibid., p. 200.

9. Letter from Madison A. Cooper, Jr., to Jack Leggett of Boston, 19 July 1952.

CHAPTER IX

1. This memorandum and all other documents used to authenticate material on the decline of the Cooper Company, Incorporated, are in a collection at 1801 Austin Avenue, Waco, Texas, property of the Cooper Foundation.

2. Letter from S. C. Little to Madison A. Cooper, Jr., 21 February 1940. Confirmed by J. R. Milam, Sr., in resumé of president's duties prepared in 1940 for Madison A. Cooper, Jr.

3. Memorandum from Madison A. Cooper, Jr., to E. C. Barrett, 15 April 1948.

4. Letter from Kay Kimbell of Fort Worth to Madison A. Cooper, Jr., 6 October 1948.

5. *Wall Street Journal* display classified advertisement, 16 February 1949.

6. Memorandum from Madison A. Cooper, Jr., to W. H. Gohagan of the Cooper Company, Inc., 6 April 1949.

7. J. R. Milam, resumé of the Cooper Company's president's duties prepared in 1940 for Madison A. Cooper, Jr.

8. Letter from Kay Kimbell of Fort Worth to Madison A. Cooper, Jr., 2 September 1949.

9. Memorandum from Madison A. Cooper, Jr., to R. B. Hoover, 22 April 1950, based on February 1950 inquiries.

10. Letter from Kay Kimbell of Fort Worth to Madison A. Cooper, Jr., 13 June 1950.

11. Letter from Madison A. Cooper, Jr., to Kay Kimbell, 23 June 1950.

12. Cooper Company Stockholder Bulletin, 6 March 1951, p. 2.

13. Resolution signed by E. C. Barrett, 13 February 1951.

CHAPTER X

1. Madison A. Cooper, Jr., "Views of the Present Management on Can-

cellation of Mrs. H. W. Carver's Proxy," unpublished manuscript, 14 August 1951, p. 1, 1801 Austin Avenue, Waco, Texas.

2. Madison A. Cooper, Jr., memorandum prepared after long distance call to Kay Kimbell temporarily in South Texas, 26 August 1951.

3. Madison A. Cooper, Jr., memorandum prepared for announcement of change in company control.

4. Letter from Madison A. Cooper, Jr., to J. R. Milam, Jr., 5 December 1951. Under Texas law all stockholders have the right to inspect corporation records at all reasonable times.

5. Madison A. Cooper, Jr., summary of three-man conference, 25 January 1952, held at 1801 Austin Avenue.

6. Madison A. Cooper, Jr., memorandum on conference with Hilton E. Howell, 13 February 1952.

7. *Directors' Minutes,* The Cooper Company, Inc., Vol. II, pp. 37–38.

8. Similar in composition and content to actual headlines appearing in the *Waco News-Tribune* and *Times-Herald* from 18 May through 17 July 1952. News story excerpts are modifications of those actually prepared by newsmen Chris Whitcraft and John Banta.

CHAPTER XI

1. Letter from Austin G. Olney of Boston, Mass., to Madison A. Cooper, Jr., 29 May 1951.

2. Letter from Olney to Cooper, 14 November 1951.

3. Cooper, *Sironia, Texas,* 1:328.

4. Ibid., 2:1048.

EPILOGUE

1. Trustees never attempted any such arrangement for two reasons: the first and second floors are so connected that neither the foundation offices above nor groups meeting below would have full privacy; although extensive remodeling could eliminate this contingency, such an expense seemed ill advised due to numerous meeting sites opened in Waco since Madison Cooper wrote these words.

2. Madison Cooper, who disliked public notice of his *personal* benefactions, encouraged full public disclosure of Cooper Foundation status and grants. A plainly visible, but unostentatious, acknowledgement of the source of Cooper Foundation capital gifts is always posted on such structures, equipment, etc. The foundation's annual report publishes its complete annual audit and numerous other details of the foundation's work and corpus. All communications media are encouraged to divulge foundation grants and such other items of community interest as Madison Cooper Day proclaimed annually by the Waco city council.

DATE DUE

GAYLORD			PRINTED IN U.S.A.